MONEY

WE MUST content ourselves with that which is within our reach; and that which cannot be approached by logical inference let us leave to him who has been endowed with that great and divine influence, expressed in the words: "Mouth to mouth do I speak with Him."

From Maimonides (1135–1204),

A Guide for the Perplexed

MONEY

BY

Lawrence S. Ritter
&
William L. Silber

BASIC BOOKS, INC., PUBLISHERS

NEW YORK   LONDON

FOR

Bella and Irving Ritter

AND

Lillian F. Silber

a mother, a father,

and a wife

all of whom deserve their share

of the blame

CONTENTS

PART I

IN THE BEGINNING

PART I

In the Beginning

1

A BOOK FOR

THE CURIOUS

In 1931, Babe Ruth received a salary of $80,000 from the New York Yankees. In 1969, Willie Mays was paid $125,000 by the San Francisco Giants. Who was better off? After income taxes, Ruth's take-home pay was $68,500, while Mays wound up with "only" $45,000. In addition, consumer prices in 1969 were about two and a half times higher than they were in 1931. At 1969 prices, Mays's $45,000 take-home pay could only buy what $18,000 would have bought in 1931. Compare $68,500 with $18,000: Ruth's salary, in terms of take-home purchasing power, was worth almost four times Mays's.

Most of this differential clearly is due to today's higher tax rates. But even if we ignore taxes, Ruth was better off. With today's cost of living about two and a half times higher than in 1931, Mays's $125,000 could buy only the real goods and services that $50,000 could purchase in 1931. Even forgetting about taxes, Babe Ruth's real income was 60 per cent larger than Willie Mays's—$80,000 compared with $50,000.

All of this is not intended to demonstrate that Babe Ruth was a better baseball player than Willie Mays (which he was), but that inflation distorts economic relationships. Willie Mays will make do, inflation or no inflation, but for most people rising prices are a more serious matter. As your income goes up, you may think you are earning more and moving up the ladder, but if prices are rising faster it is a mirage. You may be earning more dollars, but each dollar is worth less and less, so that after all is said and done you are no better off (and maybe worse) than you were before.

What does all this have to do with money? It is widely believed that increases in the price level are synonymous with increases in the money supply. The reason for this book is to explore precisely and thoroughly the influence of money on the economy: How it affects the price level, what it does to the volume of employment, whether it enhances or inhibits economic growth. In short, this is a book about money and monetary policy.

Other questions also spring to mind. Is money responsible for the ups and downs of stock prices? Why is the housing industry apparently so susceptible to changes in monetary policy? Are high interest rates always harmful to the economy? Is gold an essential part of our monetary system or a vestigial remnant of bygone days? If the money supply has such potential importance, who is responsible for determining how much of it we have—the president of the United States or the chairman of the Board of Governors of the Federal Reserve System?

These questions have been highlighted in recent years by the rebirth of monetary policy as an instrument of national economic policy, and also by widely publicized debates between the Monetarists (remember Milton Friedman?) and the Keynesians (if you forgot who John Maynard Keynes was, Paul Samuelson will do). The Monetarists are the standard-bearers of monetary policy and the Keynesians the champions of fiscal policy. In 1969, for example, great controversy arose between them as to whether the inflation could best be stopped by exclusive reliance on monetary policy or by extension of the income tax surcharge, a tool of fiscal policy.

We will explore the secrets of money and monetary policy in the following way. Part I lays the foundations for understanding problems of the sort we have mentioned above. In particular, Chapters 2 and 3 deal with the essentials of money and its relationship to the overall economy. With the tools developed in these two chapters, we face the problem of inflation head-on in Chapter 4. In Chapter 5, we turn to the crucial debate between the Monetarists and the Keynesians. How does this theoretical confrontation lead to alternative policy recommendations for solving real-world problems? In Chapter 6, we take a cold and precise look at the impact of monetary policy on the economy as a whole and on its various subsectors. Chapters 7 and 8 deal with the execution of monetary policy and the power structure that oversees it.

Building on these foundations, Part II turns to the influence of monetary policy on housing, the role of money in the stock market, and the never-ending curiosity about the services or disservices of gold. We also examine other specific issues, such as remedies for our balance-of-payments deficit, the implications of the astounding growth of financial institutions in the postwar period, and the relationship between interest rates and economic activity.

Part III returns to broader-based problems and controversies. Is the panacea for all our economic ills monetary policy or fiscal policy? Is there any rationale for the national debt ranking so high on the Worry Meter scale? Is there really a "Golden Rule" for monetary policy, as some economists would have us believe? And what will money and the financial system look like in the twenty-first century?

This is not a long book. Perhaps it is even too short to do full justice to the ground it covers. Nevertheless, after you finish it, we hope you will be more informed about money and its role in economic life, and more capable of satisfying your curiosity about what is happening today and what is likely to happen tomorrow in the sphinx-like world of monetary policy.

2

ALL THAT GLITTERS

Not too many years ago—say forty-five or so—no one would have thought of writing a book about monetary policy. Who needed it? Money, as everyone knew, depended on gold. And the economy, as everyone also knew, depended on itself. Monetary policy was unnecessary and irrelevant. Not to mention irreverent. Flanked by the twin eternal verities—the gold standard and the balanced budget—laissez faire reigned supreme.

Back then it was generally assumed that aggregate spending on the nation's output of new goods and services—the economy's gross national product (GNP)—might occasionally fluctuate somewhat. However, it was expected that such fluctuations in spending and GNP would be moderate and not too disturbing, provided the government maintained the gold standard, balanced the budget, and thereafter kept out of the way. The economy, it was widely believed, was inherently stable. Left alone, it would automatically generate the right amount of spending to produce full employment, stable prices, a high rate of economic growth, balance in international payments . . . and virtually anything else you might like to add to the list.

> Those were the days, my friend,
> We thought they'd never end.*

*Those Were The Days, Gene Raskin. TRO © 1962, 1968 by Essex Music, Inc.

But they did. There are still some whose faith in the eternal verities remains pure and unshaken; Roosevelt's finagling is to blame for the Great Depression and his abandonment of gold is responsible for the subsequent inflation. For most people, however, the issue now is not *whether* the government should intervene—but how, when, and to what extent.

The means that are most frequently used today are monetary policy (the subject matter of this book) and fiscal policy. The ends are not particularly new—high employment, price stability, economic growth, and balance-of-payments equilibrium—but the means are. Do the ends justify the means? Very few people still equate paper money with rampant inflation, unbalanced budgets with creeping socialism, and Keynes with Marx. But the emotional content of the argument has not disappeared. It has merely moved next door—to the debate between the Monetarists and the Keynesians, between monetary policy versus fiscal policy, and to controversy over the execution of monetary policy.

As a first approximation, monetary policy is concerned with regulating the money supply in order to achieve the goals of national economic policy. Similarly, fiscal policy deals with changes in government spending and tax rates for the same purposes. We will return to fiscal policy later in the book. First, however, let us set the framework for our main concern—money and monetary policy.

The Supply of Money

How large a money supply should we have in the United States? What, in fact, do we mean by the term *money* to begin with?

Money is whatever is generally accepted as a means of payment or in settlement of debts. The Indians used beads, the Eskimos used fishhooks, and we use checks and currency. On that basis, the money supply in this country amounts to almost $200 billion, roughly $150 billion in demand deposits (checking accounts) at commercial banks and about $50 billion in currency (bills and coins).

A few economists, notably Milton Friedman, also include savings deposits at commercial banks in the money supply. He argues that while a savings deposit cannot be used directly as a means of payment, since checks cannot be written on it, such deposits are so easily converted into cash that they should be counted as money. If we do add savings deposits at commercial banks, the money supply doubles to $400 billion. On similar grounds, other economists include deposits at mutual savings banks and deposits (usually called shares) in savings and loan associations as well, which would add another $200 billion to make a grand total of $600 billion.

However, most economists prefer the narrow definition of the money supply, simply the $200 billion of demand deposits and currency, because that and only that is what is generally accepted as a means of payment. Throughout this book we will use this definition. Now that we know what money is, the question still remains: How much of it should there be?

In theory, the answer is simple enough; we should have enough money so that we buy, at current prices, all the goods and services the economy is able to turn out. If we spend less, we will have idle capacity and idle men. If we spend more, we will wind up with higher prices but no more real goods or services. We need a money supply, in other words, that is large enough to generate sufficient spending to produce a

GNP that represents full employment at stable prices. Less spending would mean recession and more would mean inflation.

In practice, however, the answer is not quite so simple. Precisely how much money will give us that appropriate volume of spending? The answer is not clear, because any given amount of money can conceivably be spent more or less rapidly, thereby generating a rather wide range of potential spending. In brief, the velocity of money, its rate of turnover, is as important as the supply. It is so important, in fact, that we will devote all of Chapter 3 to the velocity of money and its implications.

Where, in all of this, does gold fit in? The amount of gold in the country is only about $10 billion. With just $10 billion in gold, how do we get $200 billion of money? Not too difficult—we just create it out of thin air under governmental supervision. In 1968, the last remaining link between the money supply and gold was severed, when the law requiring a 25 per cent gold backing behind most of our currency was repealed. If that is all news to you, it is a good indication of just how important the connection between gold and money has always been, at least in our lifetime.

Both demand deposits and currency can be increased (or decreased) without any relation whatsoever to gold. Does that disturb you? Does it lead you to distrust the value of your money? Then send it to us. We will be delighted to pay you ninety cents on the dollar, which should be a bargain if you believe all you read about a dollar being worth only fifty-seven cents, or forty-three cents, or whatever the latest figure might be.

If gold is not the watchdog, what is? What supervision is there over the creation (and destruction) of money? In other words, who controls and formulates monetary policy?

The Central Bank and Money Creation

The monetary authority in most countries is called the central bank. A central bank does not deal directly with the public; it is rather a bank for banks, and is responsible for the execution of national monetary policy. In the United States the central bank is the Federal Reserve System, created by Congress in 1913. It consists of twelve regional Federal Reserve Banks, scattered throughout the country, and a Board of Governors in Washington. This hydra-headed Monster, which some view as benign but others consider an ever-lurking peril, possesses ultimate authority over the money supply.

As noted above, the money supply consists of currency and checking accounts. Currency is manufactured by money factories—the United States Bureau of Engraving and Printing and the United States Mint—and then shipped under rather heavy guard to the Treasury and the Federal Reserve for further distribution. For the most part it enters circulation when people and business firms cash checks at their local banks. Thus it is the public that ultimately decides what proportion of the money supply will be in the form of currency, with the Federal Reserve wholesaling the necessary coins and paper to the banks. The Federal Reserve is not particularly concerned with the fraction of the money supply that is in one form or another, but rather with the *total* of demand deposits plus currency.

Money that is in the form of demand deposits, and that is three-quarters of it, comes into being when commercial banks extend credit—that is, when they make loans or buy securities. It vanishes, as silently as it came, when banks contract credit—when bank loans are repaid or banks sell securities. It is precisely here, through its ability to control the behavior of commercial banks, that the Federal Reserve wields its primary authority over the money supply and thereby implements monetary policy. This process of money creation by the banks under the influence of the Federal Reserve is sufficiently important and complex to deserve further explanation.

When a bank makes a loan to a consumer or business firm, it typically creates a checking account for the borrower's use. For example, when you borrow $1,000 from your friendly neighborhood bank, it will take your IOU and give you a checking account in return. From the commercial bank's point of view, it has an additional $1,000 of assets (namely, your IOU); this is matched by an additional $1,000 of liabilities (namely, your checking account). You could, of course, ask for $1,000 in ten-dollar bills right then and there, stuff them in your wallet, and depart. But more likely you would be equally satisfied with the demand deposit, because by writing checks on it you can make payments just as well as with currency. The creation of this $1,000 in bank demand deposits means that the money supply has increased by $1,000.

Similarly, when a bank buys a corporate or government bond, it pays for it by opening up a checking account for the seller. Assume you are holding a $1,000 corporate or government bond in your investment portfolio, and you need cash. You might sell the bond to your local bank, and the bank would add $1,000 to your checking account. Once again, from the point of view of the bank, its assets (bonds) and liabilities (demand deposits) have gone up by $1,000. Just as in the case of the bank loan, money has been created; the supply of money in the economy has increased by $1,000.

Conversely, when you repay a bank loan the bank gives you back your IOU and at the same time lowers your demand-deposit balance. If a bank sells a bond to an individual, the same reduction in demand deposits occurs. The supply of money declines. To repeat: Banks create money (demand deposits) when they lend or buy securities and destroy money when their loans are repaid or they sell securities.

Can they do this without limit? Is there any control over their ability to create and destroy money? No they can't and yes there is, and that is where the Federal Reserve comes into the picture.

A commercial bank cannot always expand its demand-deposit liabilities by making loans or buying securities. Commercial banks that are "members" of the Federal Reserve System, and they include those that do most of the banking business, must hold reserves against their demand-deposit liabilities—the current requirement is reserves of about 15 per cent against demand deposits. *These reserves must be held in the form of vault cash or as a deposit in their regional Federal Reserve Bank.* Therefore, only if a commercial bank has "excess" reserves, reserves over and above its requirements, can it create new demand deposits by making loans and buying securities. Once a bank is loaned up, with no more excess reserves, its ability to create money ceases. And if it has deficient reserves, not enough to support its existing deposits, the bank must somehow get additional reserves. Otherwise, it has no choice but to call in loans or sell securities in order to bring its deposits back in line with its reserves. If a bank has demand deposits of $10,000 but only $1,400 in reserves, it would be $100 short of meeting its required reserves. One way to set itself right with the Federal Reserve would be to call in $667 worth of loans. This would reduce its demand deposits to $9,333, at which level its $1,400 of reserves satisfies the legal 15 per cent requirement.

It is through the fulcrum of these reserves that the Federal Reserve influences commercial bank lending and investing and thereby the money supply. The Federal Reserve manipulates the reserves of the banking system and the amount of demand deposits which they can support in several different ways. In the first place, within prescribed limits established by Congress, the Federal Reserve can specify the reserve-requirement percentage. Lowering the percentage, say from 15 to 10 per cent, will instantly and automatically increase banks' excess reserves, enabling banks to make more loans (or buy securities) and to expand demand deposits. If reserve requirements were lowered from 15 to 10 per cent, the bank with the $100 reserve deficiency would suddenly find itself with $400 in excess reserves. Raising the percentage, say to 20 per cent, will just as quickly reduce excess reserves or create deficiencies, pressuring banks to call in loans (or sell securities), thereby reducing demand deposits.

Second, through facilities available for "discounting," member banks can temporarily borrow reserves from their regional Federal Reserve Bank at a price (the discount rate). For example, the problem bank, with demand deposits of $10,000 but only $1,400 in reserves, could avoid the embarrassment of having to call in loans if it were willing to borrow the needed $100 in reserves from its regional Federal Reserve Bank. The ability to borrow these reserves means that the money supply can remain unchanged. A bank could also take the initiative and borrow additional reserves to make *new* loans and thereby *increase* the money supply. The Federal Reserve influences the willingness of banks to borrow reserves by manipulating the rate it charges on such loans. A lower discount rate will tend to make borrowing reserves more attractive to the commercial banks, and a higher rate will tend to make it less attractive.

Third, and most important of all as a means of day-to-day policy-making, the Federal Reserve can buy or sell government securities (open-market operations), thereby enlarging or diminishing bank reserves. About $170 billion worth of marketable government securities are held as investments by the public—by individuals, corporations, financial institutions, and so on. These government securities came into being when the United States Treasury had to borrow to finance past budget deficits. Some are long-term bonds, running twenty or thirty years until maturity, and others are shorter-term, all the way down to government securities that are issued for only a few months which are called treasury bills. The existence of this pool of widely held marketable securities, with many potential buyers and sellers, offers an ideal vehicle through which the Federal Reserve can affect bank reserves.

When the Federal Reserve *buys* government securities in the open market, much as you would buy a stock or a bond on one of the stock exchanges, it pays for them with a check drawn on itself; when the seller deposits that check in a commercial bank, the bank's deposits at the Federal Reserve Bank—its reserves—increase. With more reserves, the bank can make loans and increase its demand deposits.

Take the following concrete example. When the Federal Reserve buys $1,000 in government securities from an insurance company (or from any individual, for that matter), it pays the insurance company with a $1,000 check drawn on itself. When the insurance company deposits the check in its commercial bank, a demand deposit of $1,000 is created for it, and the bank now has the Federal Reserve's check as an asset. This bank, in turn, presents the check for payment at its local Federal Reserve Bank and receives in exchange reserves equal to $1,000, the amount of the check. So far, the money supply has gone up by $1,000, and the bank has additional reserves. On the basis of these additional reserves, the banking system can now create *more* demand deposits by making new loans.

But what the central bank giveth the central bank can taketh away. If the Federal Reserve *sells* government securities out of its portfolio, it *receives* a check for them, drawn on some commercial bank; the Federal Reserve collects by reducing that bank's deposit at the Federal Reserve Bank, thus diminishing the bank's reserves. Result: The money supply and bank reserves both fall.

Note that the Federal Reserve could achieve the same ends—that is, change the money supply and bank reserves— by buying or selling any financial asset, any type of bond or stock. The reason for limiting its open-market operations to the purchase and sale of government securities is quite obvious; who would determine whether the Federal Reserve should buy General Motors stock or IBM? The Federal Reserve is smart enough, at least in this respect, to keep its hands out of the public hair.

To summarize: These techniques—setting reserve requirements, varying the discount rate, and open-market operations —put the reserves of the commercial banking system (and their demand-deposit potential) pretty tightly under the control of the Federal Reserve, thereby giving it sufficient leverage with which to control the money supply.

But does it really matter? What difference does it make whether the money supply increases or decreases?

Does Money Matter?

We have come full circle, back to the question that started us off: How much money should we have in the United States? What effects does monetary policy have on the economy?

Monetary policy consists of varying the amount of money

in the economy, presumably increasing it during a recession in order to encourage spending, and decreasing it (or at least increasing it at less than the normal rate) during a boom in order to inhibit spending. But whether just changing the money supply really does influence people's spending is not immediately that obvious.

Many appear to believe that monetary policy affects people's wealth and in that fashion influences their spending. Clearly, if people have more money and less of nothing else, they are wealthier and will probably spend more. But *pure* monetary policy—that is, monetary policy alone, without any accompanying fiscal policy (such as a budget deficit)— usually does *not* alter people's wealth.

An expansion in the money supply via pure monetary policy, for example, usually does not increase wealth, because the public gives up an asset or incurs a liability as part of the very process through which currency or demand deposits rise. If the money supply is increased by Federal Reserve open-market purchases of securities, the increased demand deposit acquired by the public is offset by the reduction in its holdings of government securities (they were purchased by the Federal Reserve). In any subsequent expansion in demand deposits by bank lending or security purchases, the public acquires an asset (demand deposits) but either creates a liability against itself in the form of a bank loan or sells to the bank an asset of equal value, such as a government bond. (This ignores any effects on bank profits and the value of bank stocks.)

What a change in the money supply *does* do is alter not the wealth but the *liquidity* of the public. Money is the most liquid of all assets. A liquid asset is something that can be turned into cash—that is, can be sold or "liquidated"— quickly with no loss in dollar value. Money already *is* cash. You can't get more liquid than that!

Since monetary policy by itself *can* alter the liquidity of the public's portfolio of total assets—including, in that balance sheet, holdings of real as well as financial assets—it should thereby lead to portfolio readjustments that involve spending decisions. An increase in the money supply implies that the public is more liquid than formerly; not necessarily wealthier, but more liquid. A decrease in the money supply implies that the public is less liquid than before. If the public was satisfied with its previous holdings of money relative to the rest of its portfolio, now that it has more money there will presumably be repercussions throughout the rest of its portfolio.

In other words, these changes in liquidity should lead to more (or less) spending on either real assets (cars and television sets) or financial assets (stocks and bonds). If spending on real assets expands, this means an increased demand for goods and services and GNP is directly affected. If spending on financial assets goes up, the increased demand for stocks and bonds drives up securities prices. Higher securities prices mean lower interest rates.* The fall in interest rates may induce more spending on housing and plant and equipment

---

* To avoid falling into the well-known Galbraithian footnote phobia ("no footnotes are sillier than footnotes"—John Kenneth Galbraith, *The Great Crash* [Boston: Houghton Mifflin, 1961], p. xxiii), we hereby offer our one and only:

Since it comes up again and again, it is worth devoting a moment to the *inverse* relationship between the *price* of an income-earning asset and its effective *rate of interest* (or yield). For example, a long-term bond that carries a fixed interest income of $10 a year, and costs $100, yields an annual interest rate of 10 per cent. However, if the price of the bond were to rise to $200, the effective rate of interest would drop to 10/200 or 5 per cent. And if the price of the security were to fall to $50, the yield would rise to 10/50 or 20 per cent. Conclusion: A rise (or fall) in the price of a bond is reflected, in terms of sheer arithmetic, in an automatic change in the opposite direction in the effective rate of interest. To say the price of bonds rose or the rate of interest fell are but two different ways of saying the same thing.

(investment spending), thereby influencing GNP through that route.

Whether a change in the supply of liquidity actually does influence spending or not depends on what is happening to the demand for liquidity. If the supply of money is increased but the demand for money expands even more, the additional money will be held and not spent. Easy or tight money is not really a matter of increases or decreases in the money supply in an absolute sense; rather, it is increases or decreases relative to the demand for money. In the past decade, we have had few periods in which the money supply actually decreased, yet we have had many periods of tight money because the demand rose faster than the supply.

This returns us once again to the speed with which money is spent, its rate of turnover or velocity, the subject of Chapter 3. In subsequent chapters, we will delve deeper into the influence of money and monetary policy on the economy.

3

MONEY IN ACTION

When the Federal Reserve increases the money supply by $1 billion, how does it know how much of an effect this will have on people's spending and thereby on GNP? Say we are in a recession, with GNP $20 billion below prosperity levels. Can the Federal Reserve induce a $20 billion expansion in spending by increasing the money supply by $2 billion? Or will it take a $10 billion . . . or a $15 billion . . . increase in the money supply to do the job? If people always respond in a consistent manner to an increase in their liquidity (the proportion of money in their portfolio), the Federal Reserve will be able to gauge the impact on GNP of a change in the money supply. But if people's spending reactions vary unpredictably when there is a change in the money supply, the central bank will never know whether it should increase the money supply a little or a lot (or even at all!) to bring about a specified change in spending.

Clearly, this is the key puzzle the Federal Reserve must solve if it is to operate effectively. After all, the central bank is not in business to change the money supply just for the sake of changing the money supply. Money is only a means to an end, and the end is the total volume of spending (GNP); when the chips are down, GNP will determine whether the overall economy is performing well or poorly.

How stable is the public's propensity to spend on goods and services out of increased liquidity? Does the public react to a change in the money supply predictably enough to allow the central bank to calculate the effect of its actions on GNP? Or is the reaction so unpredictable that the Federal Reserve can do no more than probe and pray?

The Missing Link

When the money supply increases, the recipients of this additional liquidity probably spend some of it on goods and services, increasing GNP. The funds thereby move from the original recipients to the sellers of the goods and services. Now *they* have more money than before, and if they behave the same way as the others, they too are likely to spend some of it. GNP thus rises further—and at the same time the money moves on to a still different set of owners who, in turn, may also spend part of it, thereby increasing GNP again.

Over a period of time, say a year, a multiple increase in spending and GNP could thus flow from the initial increase in the stock of money. Whether this expansion in GNP is large or small, relative to the change in the money supply that set it going initially, depends on two things: first, on how much of the new money is respent (passed on) at each stage; and second, on how quickly the respending takes place. If a large fraction of the increased money is respent by each recipient soon after he receives it, GNP will expand a great deal relative to the increase in the stock of money. On the other hand, if a small fraction (or none) of the increased money is respent, or if it is held a long time at each stage, the expansion in GNP during the year will be quite small relative to the enlarged money supply.

This relationship between the increase in GNP over a period of time and the change in the money supply that brought it about is important enough to have a name: the velocity of money. Technically speaking, it is found, after the process has ended, by dividing the total increase in GNP by the increase in the money supply that started it all.

We similarly can compute the velocity of the *total* amount of money in the country by dividing total GNP (not just the increase in it) by the total money supply. This gives us the average number of times each dollar turns over to buy goods and services during the year. In 1969, for example, with a GNP of $925 billion and a money supply of $195 billion, the velocity of money was 925 divided by 195 or 4.74 per annum. Each dollar, on the average, was spent about 4¾ times in purchasing goods and services during 1969.

With this missing link—velocity—now in place, we can reformulate the problem of the Federal Reserve more succinctly. The Federal Reserve controls the supply of money. Its main job is to regulate the flow of spending. The flow of spending, however, depends not only on the supply of money but also on that supply's rate of turnover or velocity, which the Federal Reserve does not have under its thumb. Since any given supply of money might be spent faster or slower—that is, velocity might rise or fall—a rather wide range of potential spending could conceivably flow from any given stock of money.

The *ideal* situation for the central bank is a stable velocity, or at least one that is changing slowly and predictably over time. If velocity is stable, or close to it, the Federal Reserve can induce virtually any volume of spending it wants simply by adjusting the money supply to the known velocity. For example, the velocity of the total money supply is now about 4¾. If an *addition* to the money supply also turns over 4¾ times a year in the purchase of goods and services, then the Federal Reserve knows for sure that if it increases the money supply by a billion dollars the end result will be an increase in GNP of $4¾ billion. In that case, the Federal Reserve has it made; monetary policy alone would be both necessary *and sufficient* to control aggregate spending.

At the other extreme, the *worst* situation from the point of view of the monetary authorities is if velocity fluctuates randomly or perversely. If velocity moves randomly, up and down without rhyme or reason, it would be impossible to gauge the impact on GNP that might result from a change in the money supply. If movements in velocity are perverse, that would mean that every time the Federal Reserve increased the money supply by 5 per cent, velocity would respond by falling 5 per cent. Monetary policy would be impotent. Changes in the money supply would merely be offset by an opposite change in velocity, leaving spending and GNP unaltered. The public would not be responding to changes in liquidity and would be deciding by itself how much it would spend, irrespective of the actions of the Federal Reserve. Under such circumstances, monetary policy would be close to useless as a tool of national economic policy.

Living with Velocity

The facts are that velocity is not perfectly stable. Unfortunately for the Federal Reserve, it does not operate in a world designed for its own convenience. But all is not necessarily lost: While velocity is not fixed, neither do its movements appear to be random or perverse. If the Federal Reserve could discover the underlying determinants of fluctuations in velocity, it might still be able to coexist with such a moving target.

With that in mind, examining the past may provide a clue to developments in the future. The velocity of the total money supply reached a peak of four in 1919, when GNP was $80 billion and the money supply $20 billion. It fell slightly during most of the 1920's and then regained that peak of four in 1929. Thereafter, during the depression and World War II, velocity fell almost continuously to an all-time low of two in 1946. In that year GNP was about $210 billion and the money supply $105 billion; each dollar, on the average, was being spent only twice.

Since then, however, velocity has risen considerably. It rose to 2.5 by 1950 . . . to 3 by 1955 . . . 3.5 in 1960 . . . 4 (the previous peak) in 1964 . . . 4.5 in 1967 . . . and now it is approaching an annual rate of turnover of 5. The increase since World War II has been steady and even, with only slight dips now and then to interrupt an otherwise unbroken upward climb.

But, of course, facts alone do not speak for themselves. Understanding requires interpretation. Why has velocity behaved this way, especially in the past quarter century? After the war it was generally expected that velocity would accelerate somewhat. Unexpected, however, has been the magnitude of the increase and its duration.

Perhaps the main reason for the extent of the postwar rise in velocity has been the increasing attractiveness of financial assets *other than money*—bonds as well as stocks, savings and loan shares as well as savings accounts in commercial banks—as prudent and desirable outlets in which to invest excess cash. These assets are often highly liquid, almost as liquid as money, and yet they possess an attribute money lacks—the right to receive an interest income. Attractive yields on financial assets other than money have led more and more people to wonder why they should ever hold any idle cash aside from what they need for day-to-day transactions purposes. And traditional concepts about how much cash-on-hand is really necessary for doing business have also come under reexamination. If cash for day-to-day transactions purposes can be pared down, then some of it can be loaned out to earn interest. The money that is put to work earning interest moves to borrowers who can use it for current purchases. As a result, a larger volume of current spending flows from the same stock of money.

Corporate treasurers, in particular, have found that it pays dividends to scrutinize their cash holdings intensively. Could they manage to get along with somewhat less in the till than they had previously thought of as "normal," and invest a portion in high-yielding time deposits at commercial banks or in U.S. treasury bills (short-term government securities)? Increasingly, the answer has been "yes," and imaginative new techniques of cash management have been developed to facilitate the process (also some not so imaginative old techniques, such as becoming "slow payers" when bills come due).

Nor has this trend escaped the attention of consumers. They have learned to economize on money by substituting lines of credit at retail stores and financial institutions in place of cash reserves; in addition, the growing use of credit cards has drastically reduced household needs for day-to-day transactions money. What was formerly held in the form of non-interest-bearing demand deposits or currency, for emergency use or for current payments, now shifts to interest-bearing savings deposits.

In conclusion, it is clear that velocity has not been stable; however, neither has it fluctuated randomly or perversely. There is a discernible pattern in the movements of velocity during the postwar period—a persistent long-run upward climb with minor short-run dips during recessions. Even though we may not be able to pinpoint all the specific determinants, we can still indicate broad cause-and-effect relationships.

Higher interest rates clearly lead to an increase in velocity by inducing business firms and households to economize on money. They hold less, lend out the excess, and others (the borrowers) can then spend it. Once learned, techniques of cash management are not easily forgotten, so that even in recessions, when interest rates fall, velocity does not drop back very far.

Furthermore, the long-run upward trend in velocity over the past quarter century suggests that fundamental structural relationships between the money supply and the spending habits of the community are apparently in the process of transition. New payment methods are developing (credit cards are a prime example), as financial innovation occurs side by side with technological innovation in industry. Such financial innovation, however, rarely takes root overnight. Established payment habits are likely to change only gradually over time.

Thus, although velocity is not fixed, neither is it likely to change drastically in the short run. The Federal Reserve may be able to live with it, even though it is a moving target. By gaining further insight into what makes velocity move, the central bank can establish a range of probabilities as to where velocity is likely to be tomorrow and the day after, and act on that basis. In other words, a morning line on velocity (not unlike the one your local bookie puts out on the races at

Hialeah)—provided the odds are unemotionally calculated and continuously reassessed in the light of emerging evidence—might still enable the Federal Reserve to come out a winner.

4

IS MONEY THE

INFLATION CULPRIT?

A short while ago, a New York restaurant celebrated its one hundredth anniversary by serving dinner on the basis of its original 1868 menu, including its 1868 prices. The most popular meal proved to be the five-course dinner for twelve cents. It included sausage (four cents), soup (two cents), liver with salad and potato (three cents), pie (two cents), and coffee (one cent). In twenty-degree weather, over 1,000 people waited in line up to three hours to get in.

Needless to say, prices today are quite different even from what they were only twenty-five years ago. Workers and businessmen, whose incomes have risen along with the rising prices of the past quarter century, are able to afford a good meal even at today's prices. But inflation is a more serious matter for many others, especially for the elderly and for retired or disabled people whose income is more or less fixed for the rest of their lives. At a sustained annual increase of 3 per cent, prices will double every twenty-four years; at an increase of 4 per cent, they will double every 17½ years; and if prices were to go up at the rate of 5 per cent annually, they would double every fourteen years. Under such circumstances, it is obvious that retirement incomes of a fixed dollar amount gradually melt away. A retirement income that is initially adequate slowly becomes marginal, and, as the years continue to unfold, it approaches the level of sheer subsistence. About the only thing many older people can hope for is that they do not live too long.

Who is responsible for inflation? Is money the culprit? Can we bring an inflationary spiral to a halt if we clamp down on the money supply?

Too Much Money Chasing Too Few Goods

The classic explanation of inflation is that "too much money is chasing too few goods." The diagnosis implies the remedy; stop creating so much money and inflation will disappear.

Such a diagnosis has indeed been accurate, painfully so, during those hard-to-believe episodes in history when runaway inflation skyrocketed prices out of sight and plunged the value of money to practically zero. Example: Prices quadrupled in revolutionary America between 1775 and 1780, when the Continental Congress opened the printing presses and flooded the country with currency. The phrase "not worth a continental" remains to this day. Germany after World War I was even more extreme; prices in 1923 were 34 billion times what they had been in 1921. In Hungary during World War II it took 1.4 nonillion pengoes in 1946 to buy what one pengo could purchase a few years earlier (one nonillion equals 1,000,000,000,000,000,000,000,000,000,-000).

Pathological breakdowns of this sort are impossible unless they are fueled by continuous injections of new money in ever-increasing volume. In such cases, money is undoubtedly the inflation culprit, and the one and only way to stop the avalanche from gathering momentum is to slam a sharp brake on the process of money creation.

Creeping Inflation

However, hyperinflation is not what we have been experiencing in this country in recent years. During World War II, consumer prices rose by about 20 per cent. In the immediate postwar years (1945–1949), after wage and price controls were removed, they climbed another 35 per cent. None of this was unexpected or particularly unusual. Prices typically rise in wartime and immediately thereafter.

The unusual thing about World War II is not that prices rose so much during and immediately after it. What *is* unusual is that they have never declined since. Quite the contrary, prices have continued onward and upward to this day, virtually without interruption, producing the longest period of continuous inflation in American history. In all prior wars, prices had gone up during and immediately after hostilities, but then had fallen back somewhat. Not this time. In all prior peacetimes, price increases had been interrupted from time to time by occasional corrective periods of stable or declining prices. No longer.

From 1949 through 1969, the cost of living increased in every year but one (1955). The annual rate of inflation over the twenty-year period averages out at slightly more than 2 per cent per year. Its persistence, month after month, year after year, has resulted in an aggregate 50 per cent increase in the cost of living.

This is not hyperinflation. It is not like America in 1775, Germany in 1923, or Hungary in 1946. This is a different sort of animal—nibbling away doggedly, insistently, without pause, at the purchasing power of the dollar. Prices do not skyrocket, they only creep—some years 2 per cent, some years 3 or 4 per cent, but always in one direction, always up, up, up.

This type of inflation is something new. Is money the culprit here, too? Can creeping inflation, like hyperinflation, be stopped simply by clamping a lid on the money supply? To work our way around these questions, it will be helpful to examine the recent inflation process a bit more closely.

Demand Pull

We understand fairly clearly—as well as anything is understood in economics, anyway—why the price level rises when aggregate demand exceeds the limits of full capacity output. This is the orthodox inflation setting, exemplified in starkest form in wartime when we simply cannot produce enough goods and services to satisfy all would-be purchasers at existing prices. The excessive demand (in relation to the available supply) bids prices up, thereby eliminating some potential buyers and, in effect, rationing the available short supply among those able and willing to pay more.

War generates the classic form of demand-pull inflation, with competition among buyers for the available goods and services driving prices up. Men are put to work producing war goods—which are bought by the government—but the incomes they receive, unless siphoned off by higher taxes, are as available as ever for the purchase of private consumer goods and services. At the same time, the output of civilian goods is curtailed as war production takes precedence.

Part of the reason for our inability to eliminate the inching up of prices is simply that we have never really brought World War II to a complete end. An entire generation has grown up which has never fully known peace. Intermittently, in the past two decades, the financial, manpower, and matériel resources of the nation have been mobilized in an effort to produce both guns *and* butter. Budget deficits, shortages, and accelerated consumer and business buying plans have periodically converged, with the swollen aggregate demand outpacing the economy's productive capacity.

Cost Push

But that cannot be the whole story. For there have been periods of relative tranquillity, primarily in the late 1950's and early 1960's, when international tensions eased and slack developed in the economy. But even then prices continued upward, although at a somewhat more leisurely pace. For example, aggregate demand from government, business, and consumers was in no sense excessive during the years 1958 through 1964. If anything, it was rather sluggish. Unemployment averaged close to 6 per cent of the civilian labor force during that seven-year period, and frequently exceeded 7 per cent during two of the years (1958 and 1961). Nevertheless, prices inched up year after year, including those years—1958 and 1961—when unemployment and idle capacity were particularly evident. By the end of 1964, consumer prices were 10 per cent higher than they had been at the end of 1957.

Why should prices rise, as they did from 1957 through 1964, when we are far below full employment of our labor force and full capacity utilization of our industrial plant? In past years, these were the very times when prices *fell,* and the impact of prior inflation was to some extent ameliorated. Some new ingredients have evidently entered the picture since the 1930's, and drastically altered the economy's response mechanism.

One such ingredient is the economic strength of labor unions. The American Federation of Labor was founded in 1886, but the real power of trade unions to influence money-wages came with the passage of the Wagner Act and related legislation half a century later. On the basis of government encouragement of unionism as a declared principle of public policy, the expansion of the economy from the depression of the 1930's into the war boom of the 1940's carried with it an enormous growth in union membership. The ranks of organized labor jumped from 3 million members in 1933 to 9 million in 1940, and to 15 million in 1946. Today, union rolls list about 18 million members. The Taft-Hartley Act of 1947 corrected some union abuses, but put hardly a dent in their new-found power to extract wage increases in excess of productivity growth, thereby generating round after round of higher production costs.

The second new ingredient—closely related to the economic power of organized labor, although not so recent an arrival—is the substantial market power of big business. Due to the nature of modern technology, which often results in lower unit production costs as the scale of operations expands, a few large firms dominate many major manufacturing industries. Their size enables these industrial giants to exert a degree of control over their prices that would be impossible in a thoroughgoing competitive environment, thereby permitting them, to some extent, to pass cost increases on to their customers.

The third new ingredient is the Employment Act of 1946, under which the government assumed responsibility for maintaining full employment through the use of its monetary, fiscal, and related powers. According to the Employment Act, "it is the continuing policy and responsibility of the federal government to use all practicable means . . . to promote maximum employment, production, and purchasing power."

Without the support of the Employment Act, neither Big Labor nor Big Business, individually or in concert, could sustain a wage-price spiral for very long. In the absence of the Employment Act, labor would have to take more seriously the possibility that it might be jacking up money-wages too far, that excessive wage demands might force businessmen to cut back on their hiring. Businessmen would similarly have to guard against pricing themselves out of the market. But such restraints are relaxed by the presence of a full employment guarantee underwritten by Big Government, standing by to "insure prosperity" with injections of purchasing power should employment or sales decline too far.

The old-fashioned pattern of demand-pull inflation—excess aggregate demand, greater than the economy's productive capacity, pulling prices up—has not disappeared. Witness the Korean War period, the 1956–1957 episode, and Vietnam. But demand-pull (or buyers' inflation) has been joined in the postwar period by a new form of inflation—cost-push inflation. Even when aggregate demand subsides, as from 1958 through 1964, prices still rise. The pace may be slower, but the direction is the same. The distinguishing feature of cost-push or sellers' inflation is a rising price level while the economy is still well below a full employment (full capacity) rate of production.

Even when full employment is far distant on the horizon, Big Labor and Big Business start to turn the screws. Backed by substantial market (and political) power of their own, underwritten by a full employment guarantee that gives immunity—at least to some extent—from the consequences of their actions, strong unions and large corporations begin throwing their weight around and marking wages and prices up even when aggregate demand is weak and anemic. As we move closer and closer to full employment, they gradually become more aggressive until, in the immediate neighborhood of full employment, the pressure for higher wages and prices becomes literally explosive. At this point, for all practical purposes, cost and demand become virtually indistinguishable as they interact, reinforcing each other.

Indeed, it is somewhat artificial to separate the two kinds of inflation to begin with; wage increases in excess of productivity growth mean higher costs for the businessman, thereby putting upward cost pressure on prices. Those same higher wages also mean larger incomes for wage-earners, thereby generating a step-up in consumer spending which yanks prices up from the demand side. The stage is set for a new round of wage negotiations based on the increase in the cost of living, as the process feeds on itself and continues ad infinitum.

Money and Creeping Inflation

Unlike hyperinflation, money is not so clearly and uniquely the culprit when it comes to the real problem of our times, creeping inflation. The "fit" between the money supply and the cost of living exists, but it is rather loose and a bit baggy. Like a 32A girl wearing a 36C, things tend to jiggle around quite a bit.

Take, for example, the last four decades:

1. From the end of 1930 to the end of 1940, the money supply increased by 70 per cent, but prices, instead of rising, fell 15 per cent.

2. From 1940 to 1950, the money supply increased by 175 per cent, but prices rose by only 80 per cent, less than half as much.

3. From the end of 1950 to the end of 1960 provides the best fit; the money supply and the consumer price index both rose by about 20 per cent.

4. However, from 1960 through 1969 the relationship sags again; the money supply increased by 40 per cent, but prices by just 20 per cent.

Even the 20:20 relationship during the 1950's turns out to be less impressive upon closer examination. During the first half of the decade the money supply increased twice as fast as prices, while during the second half prices increased twice as rapidly as the money supply. At the end of the 1960's, the money supply was about 4½ times larger than it had been in 1940, but prices were "only" about 2½ times higher.

This is not meant to imply that money has nothing to do with creeping inflation. Quite the contrary, it has a great deal to do with it indeed, if only because, sooner or later, people simply will not be able to continue buying the same amount of goods and services at higher and higher prices unless the money supply increases. If the money supply today were no larger than it was in 1940 ($40 billion), or even than it was in 1950 ($115 billion), prices would have stopped rising long ago. Over the long run, an increase in the money supply is a *necessary* condition for the continuation of inflation, creeping or otherwise.

But it is not a *sufficient* condition. Increases in the money supply do not always result in inflation. An increase in the money supply will not raise prices if velocity falls (as in the 1930's). Even if velocity remains constant, an increase in the money supply will not raise prices if production expands. When we are in a depression, for example, the spending stimulated by an increase in the money supply is likely to raise output and employment rather than prices. Furthermore, in the short run at least, and sometimes the short run is a matter of several years, increased spending and inflation can be brought about by increases in velocity without any increase in the money supply, as we saw in Chapter 3.

Nevertheless, it bears repeating that inflation can only persist for any length of time by grace of the central bank. If the inflation is primarily demand-pull, a cutback—or merely stability—in the money supply will sooner or later reduce spending and thereby eliminate, or at least substantially moderate, the upward drift of prices. If the inflation is primarily cost-push, a cutback or stability in the money supply will sooner or later make it difficult, if not impossible, for business to sell its products at higher and higher prices—and thereby make it equally impossible for them to grant wage increases in excess of productivity growth, no matter how strong labor may be. Pursued aggressively, monetary policy undoubtedly could effectively halt price increases in most sectors of the economy.

The Trade-off between Price Stability and Employment

Since inflation is not something we want any more of, and since the tools to curb it are at hand, why don't we just use them and put a stop to these never-ending increases in the cost of living?

The reason we hesitate is because of a conflict of national objectives. The cost of price stability—in terms of the unemployment necessary to get it—is too high. If we pursued monetary (and fiscal) policies with the determination necessary to put a total and complete brake on inflation, we would probably find ourselves with unemployment of about 8 per cent of the labor force. We do not want any more inflation, but we do not want any more depressions either. And so far we have been unable to find a solution to the problem of stopping rising prices without simultaneously bringing on at least a recession.

To put the problem succinctly, we evidently cannot have both price stability and full employment at one and the same time. If we want stable prices, we have to sacrifice full employment. And if we want a high level of employment, we have to give up stable prices. Exactly what are the terms of this trade-off?

On the basis of our experience over the past dozen years, the illustration on the opposite page—known as a "Phillips Curve," after its popularizer, Professor A. W. Phillips—gives a rough idea of the cost, in terms of unemployment, of various degrees of price stability. For example, X on the chart (a 4 per cent increase in prices, 3.5 per cent unemployment) represents the situation in 1968; Y (1.2 per cent inflation, 5.7 per cent unemployment) represents 1963.

As the Phillips Curve indicates, obtaining absolute price stability would require an estimated 8 per cent unemployment rate, a rather high cost indeed. But reaching full employment (defined as consistent with 3.5 per cent unemployment, on the grounds that anything lower is totally unrealistic) would probably result in an inflation rate close to 4 per cent a year, also no small price to pay.

Furthermore (and this the chart does not indicate), for

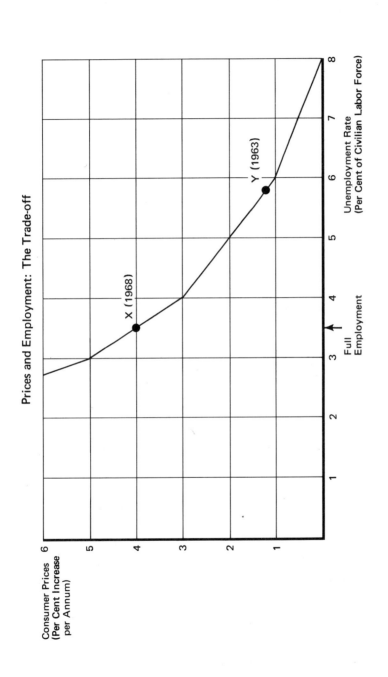

Prices and Employment: The Trade-off

well over a decade the black unemployment rate has been approximately twice the national average. An overall national unemployment rate of 8 per cent, which is about what it would take to eliminate inflation completely, implies a black unemployment rate at the deep depression level of 16 per cent. Even worse, the black teen-age unemployment rate has been averaging *seven* times the overall jobless rate for many years; an overall national unemployment rate of 8 per cent means a black teen-age unemployment rate of more than 50 per cent.

To slow down price inflation from 3 to 1 per cent a year involves an increase in overall unemployment from 4 to 6 per cent. But it means an increase in black unemployment from 8 to 12 per cent, and in black teen-age unemployment from 28 to 42 per cent. We cannot really afford to permit inflation to continue, but we can hardly afford to stop it, either.

The optimum choice among this array of less-than-happy alternatives is not amenable to a purely economic solution. If we choose high employment (say no more than 3.5 per cent unemployment), then some people will be hurt by the substantial inflation (about 4 per cent a year). On the other hand, if we move toward the lower part of the curve and choose something close to stable prices, then other people will be hurt by the heavy unemployment. An economist, as an economist, has no basis on which he can judge whether it is better to help A and hurt B, or help B and hurt A. The resolution of this conflict of interests fundamentally involves personal value judgments and assessments of the social implications of the alternatives more than it involves economics.

Most likely in the future, the political process will generate a rate of price increase and a level of overall unemployment not too different from what we have had over the past ten or fifteen years: price increases of 2 to 3 per cent a year, on average, and unemployment of 4 to 5 per cent. This will probably be bearable provided we can, by other means, bring down the black unemployment rate, adult and teen-age, to equality with the white, and adjust social security and related payments to keep pace with changes in the cost of living.

This would be far from perfection, but it could be worse. Fortunately, there is no solid evidence that creeping inflation need inevitably escalate into runaway inflation, although that possibility should certainly not be dismissed completely. However, our tax structure is too efficient and our monetary system too firmly under control for hyperinflation to be very likely. Barring vast social disintegration or major defeat in war, there is little probability that this country will become another case history in monetary pathology, like Germany or Hungary.

Instead, chances are we will continue to get just about what we have been getting—a gradual, fluctuating, but unceasing erosion of the purchasing power of the dollar. If the rate of price increase turns out to average about 2½ per cent annually over the next three decades (which is not improbable), it is somehow vaguely comforting, in a stoic sort of way, to know that in the year 2000, when we are commuting regularly to some distant planet, the cost of living here will be precisely double what it is today.

5

THE MONETARISTS

VERSUS

THE KEYNESIANS

Each baby girl and tiny man
That's born into a family nest
Is either a little Keynesian
Or else a little Monetarest.

"Those who cannot remember the past," said George Santa-yana in 1905, "are condemned to repeat it." And, he might have added, those who cannot remember the arguments of the past are condemned to repeat them as well. John Stuart Mill was a Monetarist and the Reverend Thomas Malthus was a Keynesian. The issues involved are as crucial and thought-provoking today as they were a century ago. They also have significant implications for economic growth and stability and the means we use to achieve them.

The president of the United States will use very different approaches in economic policy-making depending on whether his orientation is Keynesian or Monetarist. As a Keynesian, he and the chairman of his Council of Economic Advisers would spend considerable time pressing the Congress for countercyclical tax and expenditure legislation. If he were a Monetarist, he would expend more effort trying to influence the actions of the Federal Reserve. The Eisenhower administration had essentially a Monetarist course, while the orientation of economic policy under Kennedy and Johnson was primarily Keynesian. The Nixon administration appears to be middle of the road.

What are the underlying differences between these two schools? And how do their theoretical disputes affect their policy recommendations?

The Monetarist View

The Monetarists used to be called Quantity Theorists. Their lineage can be traced at least as far back as Jean Bodin in the sixteenth century, through John Locke, David Hume, David Ricardo, John Stuart Mill, up to Irving Fisher in the 1920's and 1930's, and now Milton Friedman in the 1960's and 1970's. Historically, they used to be concerned primarily with the relationship between the quantity of money and prices, viewing the money supply as the main determinant of the price level. The modern Quantity Theorists—or Monetarists—no longer believe changes in the money supply only affect the price level. As they see it, the role of money is much broader than that; it is the crucial determinant of GNP.

According to the Monetarists, there is a direct and reliable link between the money supply and GNP. That link is the stability of monetary velocity. Because of it, a change in the money supply will change aggregate spending and GNP by a predictable amount.

The chain of transmission from the money supply to GNP

is visualized as working roughly in the following fashion. Assume that the Federal Reserve increases the money supply through open-market purchases of government securities. This increases the liquidity of the public; they are now holding cash in place of government securities. However, people do not want simply to hold this additional money. According to the Monetarists, people only want money as a medium of exchange for day-to-day transactions purposes, or to hold temporarily preparatory to making purchases in the near future. Based on the current volume of transactions—represented by the current GNP—they already had just about the amount of money they needed. So, finding themselves with some extra money, they proceed to spend it on real assets, on real goods and services, thereby driving up GNP.

If the money supply was increased during a recession, then the increased spending primarily will raise employment and real output; on the other hand, if the economy was already close to full employment, then the increase in GNP will consist mainly of higher prices.

How high will GNP go? The answer, according to the Monetarists, is that spending on real goods and services will continue to climb until GNP has risen to the point where the relationship between it and the money supply becomes the same as it had been before the money supply was increased by the Federal Reserve. That relationship, of course, is exactly what we mean by monetary velocity (GNP/M). Once GNP has reached the point where it once again stands in its previous ratio to the money supply, then the public will finally be satisfied to hold the increased stock of money as a medium of exchange and spending will level off.

The same thing could be said in still another way. The increase in the money supply makes the public's portfolio of assets more liquid than it had been. This increased liquidity leads to the purchase of additional (less liquid) real assets until the portfolio's liquidity is restored to its former state.

A decrease in the money supply works in similar fashion, except in the opposite direction. When the Federal Reserve reduces the money supply through open-market sales of government securities, the public finds itself short of cash relative to the volume of business being done. Spending on

"Frank, how ever did you find this guru?"

goods and services contracts, driving GNP lower until the previous relationship between GNP and the (now smaller) money supply is restored. Faced with a shortage of liquidity, the public cuts back its spending until GNP drops to the point where the original ratio of GNP to the money supply is reestablished and velocity falls back to "normal." GNP will then stabilize in line with the smaller money supply.

Now it is clear where the Monetarists got their name. We saw in Chapter 3 that, from the point of view of the central bank, the ideal situation is where velocity is stable (or if it changes, that it does so gradually and predictably). This is precisely *the* main assumption of the Monetarists.

Given such conditions, the Federal Reserve can induce virtually any volume of spending it wants simply by adjusting the money supply to the known and dependable velocity. Monetary policy is both necessary *and sufficient* to control GNP. In the Monetarist World, there is no need to even pay any attention to fiscal policy (the Keynesians' pet). Changes in the money supply can do the whole job, and stabilization policy should concentrate on that and that alone. No wonder Monetarists blame the Federal Reserve whenever *anything* goes wrong!

The Keynesian View of Money

The Gospel according to Saint John—the late John Maynard Keynes—is that the channels through which the money supply affects GNP are rather different. They are less direct and also less reliable, primarily because velocity is not viewed as very stable in either the short or the long run.

The chain of transmission from the money supply to GNP is visualized as follows. Assume once more that the Federal Reserve increases the money supply by open-market purchases of government securities. Again, this increases the liquidity of the public. However, people *may* want to simply hold this additional liquidity. The entire process might end right there, before it has hardly begun. The public gets additional money and hoards it. Period. The money supply has increased but GNP is unaffected. Velocity has fallen. In the Keynesian World, unlike the Monetarist World, the public holds cash not only for day-to-day transactions purposes but *also* as idle balances or as a pool of liquidity for possible speculation in the stock and bond markets. A Monetarist, of course, would deny that this could happen, because people would not want to hold idle or speculative balances, and therefore velocity would not fall.

Suppose the Monetarists have a point: that people do *not* want to hold the additional cash. Finding themselves with more money, they proceed to spend it. In the Monetarist World they would spend it on *real* assets, on real goods and services, thereby directly driving up GNP. In the Keynesian World, however, they would spend it not on real assets but on *financial* assets, such as stocks and bonds. The prices of securities rise and interest rates fall. The increased money supply may also increase the availability of credit as well as lower its cost. But GNP still has not been affected.

This drop in interest rates and increased availability of credit *may,* then, induce some business firms or consumers to borrow and purchase real goods and services. *Finally,* GNP has been affected.

A decrease in the money supply works in similar fashion. The Federal Reserve reduces the money supply so that the public finds itself short of cash. The public may just hold less cash and that will be that. GNP will not be affected. Or the public may sell some *financial* assets (or buy less than it had been buying), driving securities prices down and interest rates up. The higher rates, and accompanying decreased availability of credit, *may* lead to less borrowing and less spending, finally reducing GNP.

To summarize the Keynesian view: A change in the money supply can only affect aggregate spending and GNP if it *first* changes interest rates and/or the availability of credit, and *then* only if business or consumer spending is sensitive to those changes. In this way of looking at things, there's many a possible slip 'twixt the cup and the lip.

It is obvious that in the Keynesian view one of the keys to the effectiveness of monetary policy is what happens to interest rates on financial instruments. Unless they change, monetary policy is probably impotent. The Monetarists, however, do not view what happens to interest rates as a major link in the sequence between monetary action and the ultimate impact on spending. In fact, according to the Monetarists, if interest rates do not change at all, it probably indicates an extremely *powerful* monetary policy, since (presumably) the entire change in liquidity is spent directly on goods and services and none at all in financial markets.

The question of the strength of monetary policy will be explored in detail in Chapter 6. Even at this point, however, it is obvious that the Monetarist view implies a very direct and certain impact of the money supply on economic activity. Increases in the supply of money will always result in a significant increase in spending. Money is only a temporary abode of purchasing power, and any increase will be spent on goods and services.

In the Keynesian way of looking at things, the link between monetary policy and economic activity is more tenuous. Increases in the money supply may or may not affect spending. It depends partly on how much money the public wants to hold idle, which in turn depends, among other things, on anticipations regarding future securities prices. Even if the public does buy securities and interest rates do fall, the impact on GNP still depends on whether businessmen will want to borrow and spend more—largely a function of their profit expectations. The Monetarist World is more mechanistic than the Keynesian one; in the Keynesian World, changes in people's expectations regarding the future course of interest rates, profits, prices, and business conditions can upset (or reinforce) the monetary applecart.

It should be noted that the Keynesians' skepticism regarding the efficacy of monetary policy is paralleled by their opposite stance on fiscal policy. Fiscal policy, as you may recall, is concerned with the manipulation of government expenditure and tax rates in order to influence economic activity. Keynesians believe that a change in government spending alters GNP directly; a change in tax rates alters consumer spending, also changing GNP. However, the Monetarists take issue with these alleged truisms of Keynesian economics. We will return to the details of fiscal policy and the arguments over its effectiveness in Chapter 15.

Is It Money or Credit?

A subsidiary but important debate between the Monetarists and the Keynesians is whether the Federal Reserve, in conducting monetary policy, should look only at the money supply or at overall credit conditions as well.

The Keynesian analysis is a *credit,* as opposed to a strictly *monetary,* chain of causation. In a sense, money per se is seen as not too important until it finds its way into the hands of a potential spender. To a Monetarist, anyone holding money is a likely spender. But to a Keynesian, a loan transaction may be necessary to move money from its current owner, who may be holding it idle, to a borrower who wants to spend it. Thus the Keynesians take a credit view, concerned with financial assets, credit availability, the direction of interest rates, the reaction of lenders and borrowers to rate changes, and the role of financial markets as conduits for funds.

To a Monetarist, all this is excess baggage, more harmful

than helpful. It is money that counts, money per se, and its effects on GNP are not roundabout but direct. To look at anything else is only a distraction.

As an illustration of a case where the two views diverge, assume that funds move from an individual to a business firm in a loan transaction (say the purchase of a newly issued corporate bond). The money supply remains the same; the corporation now has more but the individual has less. To a Monetarist, there will be no net change in spending since there has been no change in the money supply; the business firm, with more money, will increase its spending; but this will be offset by the lender, with less money, decreasing his. A Keynesian, on the other hand, would say that the result is more likely to be a net increase in spending; the lender is probably parting with what were idle balances, which in the till of the borrowing corporation will now be activated. The money supply is unchanged, but its velocity will increase.

The Federal Reserve adheres essentially to a credit, rather than a strictly monetary, approach. Indeed, it frequently shies away from the term *monetary policy* in favor of the broader *monetary and credit policy*. Open-market operations, reserve-requirement changes, and discount-rate movements affect credit conditions at least as much as they affect the money supply. Credit conditions include, among other things, interest rates on a wide variety of securities, the volume of activity in the various financial markets, bank reserve positions, credit extensions by commercial banks, and the flow of funds into and out of other financial institutions. The Federal Reserve considers all such credit conditions as well as the money supply when it decides what action it should or should not take.

In fact, for many years, the Federal Reserve's Board of Governors in Washington appeared to consider changes in the money supply only incidentally, perhaps not even on a par with other financial variables. Recently, however, prodded by the maverick Federal Reserve Bank of St. Louis, the money supply has become more prominent in Board deliberations. Nevertheless, the skeptical attitude toward excessive emphasis on the money supply is revealed by the label the Board's research staff has pinned on the St. Louis Bank's analytical framework—Brand X.

Who Is Right?

The Monetarists claim that monetary policy should be conducted only for the purpose of controlling the money supply. The Keynesians argue that interest rates and credit availability are even more significant. The Monetarists contend that changes in the money supply are the major reason for fluctuations in GNP. The Keynesians maintain that credit conditions are more important than the money supply, and, in any event, that fiscal policy is more important than either.

Ultimately, these differences can be settled only by empirical tests. As is often true in economic research, however, the factual evidence necessary to resolve the issues has been ambiguous at best and misleading at worst. There are credible (and incredible) empirical studies by eminent economists that come to diametrically opposite conclusions.

It would be easy enough to resolve the controversy if we could ascertain how portfolios are typically adjusted following a change in the money supply; the Keynesians would be correct if only financial assets are purchased, the Monetarists if only real assets are bought. In practice, it is most likely that *both* financial and nonfinancial adjustments are made when liquidity increases (or decreases). The crucial issues are which adjustments come first, which dominate, and which are the more stable behavior patterns.

In their most altruistic moments, some Monetarists are willing to admit that increased spending on financial assets may be the initial *temporary* response to an increase in the money supply. And some Keynesians will grant that a small part of an increase in the money supply may *occasionally* spill over directly into markets for goods and service. Beyond that, little progress toward reconciliation is discernible.

In Chapter 6 we will explore available evidence regarding the strength of monetary policy, and in Chapter 15 we will return to the debate. Although Monetarists and Keynesians may not be able to agree on theoretical issues, it is still possible that they might be able to reach a consensus in terms of policy. *If,* for example, most Keynesians were to conclude that a change in the money supply *does* change interest rates and/or the availability of credit, and were to conclude further that spending on goods and services *is* sensitive to those changes, then they would see monetary policy as having a significant effect on GNP; the combatants might not be as far apart in practice as they are in theory.

6

HOW EFFECTIVE IS

MONETARY POLICY?

If monetary policy is to alter **GNP** it cannot do it by mystic incantations. It has to do it by changing the consumer spending of households, the investment spending of business firms, or the expenditures of governments, either federal or state and local.

What categories of spending does monetary policy affect? To what extent? With what time lags? In contrast to the theoretical discussion of Chapter 5 and the velocity analysis of Chapter 3, the purpose of this chapter is to present the state of knowledge in this area as precisely—that is, in terms of numbers—as possible. Here are the facts.

Time Lags in Monetary Policy

By their own admission Federal Reserve officials are not omniscient. If the economy starts to slip into a recession, it takes time before the experts realize what is happening so they can take steps to correct it. Similarly, if inflation begins to accelerate, it takes a while before the evidence verifies the fact.

Prompt recognition of what the economy is doing is not as easy as it sounds. For one thing, the available data are often inadequate and frequently mixed: New car orders will rise while retail department store sales are falling; farm prices may be dropping while employment in urban areas is rising. Furthermore, the economy rarely proceeds on a perfectly smooth course, either up or down. Every upsweep is interrupted from time to time by erratic dips; every decline into recession is punctuated irregularly by false signs of progress which then evaporate. Is a change only a brief interruption of an already existing trend, or is it the start of a new trend in the opposite direction? No one is ever perfectly sure. This problem of getting an accurate "fix" on what is happening in the economy, or what is likely to happen in the near future, is called the *recognition lag* in monetary policy. In 1968–1969, for example, the Federal Reserve did not recognize that inflation was as serious a problem as it turned out to be until rising prices had gathered too much momentum to be halted.

As soon as the recognition lag ends, the *impact lag* begins, spanning the time from when the central bank starts using one of its tools, say open-market operations, until an effect is evident on the ultimate objective—aggregate spending in the economy. It may take weeks before interest rates change significantly after a monetary action has begun. Changes in credit availability also take time. And a further delay is probable before actual spending decisions are affected. Once monetary policy does start to influence spending, however, it will most likely continue to have an impact on GNP for quite a while.

Regarding the recognition lag, rough evidence suggests that the Federal Reserve generally starts to ease about half a year or more after a boom has already run its course, whereas it starts to tighten only about three months after the trough in a business cycle. This evidence is less than definitive, and it is likely that under some circumstances the monetary authorities will sense what is going on and take action more promptly than under other circumstances. Nevertheless, the inference that the central bank is typically more concerned with preventing inflation than with avoiding recession probably contains a grain of truth.

The impact lag is most conveniently discussed, along with the strength of monetary policy, in terms of the results that formal econometric models of the economy have produced. An econometric model is a mathematical-statistical representation that describes how the economy behaves. Such a model gives empirical content to theoretical propositions about how individuals and business firms, borrowers and lenders, savers and spenders react to economic stimuli. After such relationships are formalized in a mathematical expression, data on past experience in the real world are used to estimate the precise behavioral pattern of each sector. A model, therefore, is based on real-world observations jelled into a formal pattern by the grace of statistical techniques. Thrown into a computer, the model simulates the economy in action and grinds out predictions based on the formal interactions the model embodies.

Our knowledge of how best to construct such a model is still fairly rudimentary. The same data can produce different results depending on the theoretical propositions used to construct the model. A Keynesian model, for instance, would incorporate different behavioral assumptions than a Monetarist model and hence grind out an alternative set of predictions. Furthermore, the data we have available to feed in are not all that we would like. In any case, past relationships are not always reliable guides to future behavior; if they were, the favorite would always win the football game and marriages would never end in divorce.

Nevertheless, despite all their shortcomings, such models, if carefully and objectively constructed, are probably superior to casual off-the-cuff observation followed by inadequately supported generalizations. They are superior, that is, provided they are always taken with a healthy dose of skepticism.

The Federal Reserve, together with economists at the Massachusetts Institute of Technology, have developed an econometric model of the behavior of economic aggregates in the United States. Many other economists have done similar work at other universities and financial institutions. But our discussion will be based primarily on the Federal Reserve–MIT model, which was prepared specifically to evaluate the impact of stabilization policies on economic activity.

The Impact of Open-Market Operations on GNP

The magnitude of the impact of monetary policy, as well as the time lags involved, can be represented in terms of the effects of open-market operations. According to the Federal Reserve–MIT model, a Federal Reserve open-market purchase that expands bank reserves by $1 billion increases GNP by about $1 billion within six months, by about $2 billion after one year, and by nearly $8 billion after two years. At the end of one year, demand deposits will have increased by $4 billion, the treasury bill rate will have fallen by about one-half of one percentage point, and the interest rate on corporate bonds will have declined about one-fourth of one percentage point.

These results imply that there may be rather long lags in the effect of monetary actions on GNP. The impact after one year is only 25 per cent of the effect after two years. To have a significant short-run impact probably requires rather large open-market operations and changes in reserves. To get an expansion of $10 billion in GNP after one year, for instance, would require open-market purchases sufficient to increase bank reserves by $5 billion, which would raise demand deposits by $20 billion—roughly a 10 per cent increase in the money supply—and drop the treasury bill rate by a full two percentage points. In the past, the Federal Reserve has not been anxious to change the money supply by such proportions, which indicates something about the Federal Reserve or about its econometric model or both.

There is another econometric model of the economy, developed by Professors Albert Ando of the University of Pennsylvania and Stephen Goldfeld of Princeton, that incorporates more fully the availability of credit, as well as interest rates. As would be expected, the effectiveness of monetary policy is enhanced as compared with the Federal Reserve's model.

According to the Ando-Goldfeld model, to get an increase of $10 billion in GNP after one year would require an open-market purchase of only $3 billion, which would raise demand deposits by $8 billion and lower the treasury bill rate less than one-half of one percentage point. Obviously, the prognosis for monetary policy is much brighter under this model. The two versions of monetary policy's effectiveness should move closer together as the Federal Reserve builds credit-availability effects into its own computer. In fact, preliminary evidence along these lines suggests that when some credit-availability effects are included in the Federal Reserve's model, the impact of a $1 billion increase in reserves is to raise GNP by more than $5 billion after one year, as opposed to the $2 billion impact cited above.

Some economists have argued that the effectiveness of monetary policy is asymmetrical—that is, monetary policy is more effective in stopping inflation than in getting us out of a recession. They reason that the high interest rates and curtailed availability of credit that characterize tight money cannot help but force restrictions on spending, while the low interest rates and ample credit availability that are typical of easy money will not necessarily induce people to borrow and spend more.

The econometric models, however, reveal no such asymmetry. They grind out similar results, tight or easy money, except of course that the changes are all in opposite directions. The caveat, if there is one, is that the behavioral patterns built into the models are probably realistic only during "normal" times. A deep depression may so alter response mechanisms that reality will be very different from computerized predictions. The conclusion that the effects of monetary policy seem to be symmetrical during periods of normal recession or inflation is reassuring but not necessarily too helpful. The definition of a normal recession may turn out to be a contractionary phase of the business cycle in which monetary policy is effective; if monetary policy is not effective, then the recession is defined as abnormal.

Thus far we have discussed the overall impact of monetary policy on GNP but have not explored the particular categories of spending involved. Monetary policy does not have an equal impact on all types of expenditure. Which kinds of spending does it affect most, and which kinds of spending appear to be relatively immune?

Investment Spending

One would expect that an increase in interest rates should lower investment spending. If the cost of borrowing rises, business firms should be less willing to incur new debt in order to build new factories or buy new equipment. The historical record shows, however, that interest rates and business investment almost always move in the *same* direction. As in most cases where the facts contradict economic theory, one must give ground—and it is usually the facts.

In the historical record, many things are happening simultaneously, so that separate strands of cause and effect are not sorted out. Investment spending is influenced by a number of factors besides interest rates—by sales expectations, anticipated profitability, pressures from competitors who may be installing new equipment, the degree of capacity currently being utilized, the availability of internal funds (undivided profits and depreciation reserves), expectations regarding labor costs, and expectations regarding inflation, to name only some. An increase in interest rates may inhibit investment, and yet investment may, in fact, rise if a number of these other elements shift sufficiently to offset the effect of a rise in interest costs.

The actual change in investment spending from one year to the next reflects the net impact of *all* the variables influencing it, not just interest rates alone. We would expect, however, that if interest rates had not risen, investment would probably have expanded even further.

Econometric methods permit isolation of specific factors, allowing us to experiment in the "laboratory" of statistical techniques, as it were. The effects of interest rates on invest-

ment, for example, can be examined holding all other
influences constant. The results show that a rise in interest
rates does reduce investment spending. In the Federal
Reserve's model, for example, an increase of one percentage
point (say, from 5 to 6 per cent) in the corporate bond rate
lowers business spending on new plant and equipment by
about $0.5 billion after one year, by about $2.5 billion after
two years, and by $4 billion after three years.

In this instance, the time lag is clearly quite substantial. In
most cases, investment decisions are not made in the
morning and executed in the afternoon. Decisions regarding
the installation of new machinery and the construction of
new plants are usually made many months in advance of
their actual execution. Thus an increase in rates does not
promptly affect investment spending. What it does affect is
decisions currently being made about plans that will not
actually be *implemented* until months or years in the future.

The Federal Reserve–MIT model does reveal, however,
that there is one category of investment spending that is
extremely sensitive to a change in interest rates. That category is residential construction, which, although it is not
business investment, is still generally considered a form of
investment because of the long time horizon involved, with
returns accruing for many years into the future. An increase
of one percentage point in the interest rate lowers housing
expenditures by $2 billion within nine months and by $3
billion after a year. Some of the implications of this strong
relationship between monetary policy and home-building are
explored further in Chapter 11.

Small business perhaps deserves special mention in any
discussion of the impact of monetary policy on investment
expenditures. Spokesmen for small business have always
contended that during periods of tight money, commercial

banks discriminate against them in their allocation of scarce loanable funds.

The evidence on this is not altogether clear, but it is likely that small firms are indeed at a disadvantage relative to large borrowers during periods when banks are short of funds. Furthermore, large firms have access to the corporate bond market, the commercial paper market, and other alternative sources of funds, while small firms do not.

On the other hand, the extension of trade credit (delayed payment for supplies) from large to small firms tends to offset some of these disadvantages. In effect, through their supplier-customer relationships, the large firms pass their access to funds on to the smaller firms in the form of trade credit. To some extent this alleviates the problem, although it is not likely that it eliminates it.

State and Local Government Spending

Construction expenditures by state and local governments also appear sensitive to the actions of the monetary authorities. Municipal bond flotations are often reduced, postponed, or completely cancelled during periods of high and rising interest rates. Many municipal governments have self-imposed interest-rate ceilings that eliminate them from the market when rates go up. In other instances, when interest costs become too heavy, local voters become reluctant to approve bond issues for school construction and other projects, since the higher interest burden implies the immediate or eventual imposition of higher property or sales taxes.

The Federal Reserve–MIT model indicates that a one percentage point rise in the interest rate cuts state and local government spending by almost $2 billion after six months.

Subsequently, however, the impact declines as the municipalities rethink their problems and, typically, proceed sooner or later with much of their planned expenditures.

Consumer Spending

Consumption expenditures are affected by monetary policy indirectly, primarily through the effect of monetary policy on GNP which then has repercussions on consumer spending. For example, tight money raises interest rates, decreases investment spending and thereby GNP, which in turn lowers people's disposable income and hence their consumption.

Some evidence suggests a more direct link between monetary policy and one area of consumer spending, namely the purchase of consumer durables. Except that the buying is done by the household sector, economists often treat the purchase of consumer durables—automobiles, furniture, television sets—as a form of investment. Money supply and interest-rate movements do seem, to some extent, to have direct effects on consumer durable spending, although with a considerable lag (a year and a half).

One of the reasons for the minimal direct effect and the long lag is that, although open-market interest rates may be affected fairly quickly by monetary policy, rates on consumer credit tend to adjust rather sluggishly. Also, stepped up promotional and marketing efforts by retailers may offset the effects of higher rates. Sellers advertise monthly payments rather than the total cost of a consumer durable bought on time. An extension of a loan's maturity (forty months to pay instead of thirty-six months) will often keep monthly payments unchanged even though interest rates, and the total cost to the buyer, have gone up.

Lags Again

To summarize: Overall, monetary policy appears to be moderately effective in influencing the course of the economy. An open-market operation that raises long-term interest rates by one percentage point will reduce the growth in GNP by about $8 billion after a year, according to the Federal Reserve's model. Over a third of this is due to the impact on residential construction, some to business plant and equipment investment spending (with perhaps a disproportionate effect on small business), some to state and local government spending, and the remainder to the indirect effects on consumer spending, which continue to build up.

However, when the initial recognition lag is combined with the impact lags, the usefulness of monetary policy as a stabilization device becomes less obvious. Suppose a boom tops out in January but the Federal Reserve does not realize it is over until July, at which time monetary policy starts to ease. Its pre-July tightness may still be having depressing effects through the first half of the *following year,* but by then we might well be in the middle of a recession and in need of exactly the opposite medicine. The Federal Reserve, of course, will be providing that opposite medicine, but its expansionary effects may be so long delayed that they might not take hold until we are in another boom, thus once again making matters worse. Monetary policy will be a destabilizer rather than a stabilizer!

We will return to the crucial topic of lags in Chapter 17, where we discuss the optimum execution of monetary policy and assess the role it can best play in an overall stabilization program.

7

INDICATORS

AND INSTRUMENTS

The telephone number of Radio City Music Hall at Rockefeller Center is (212) 757–3100. If you call them, they will be happy to tell you what is going on this week: what picture is playing, at what times, when the stage show begins, just about everything except the personal habits of the Rockettes. The telephone number of the Board of Governors of the Federal Reserve System in Washington is (202) 737–1100. However, if you call *them* to find out what is going on, you will not learn much more than if you dialed the Central Intelligence Agency—(703) 351–1100.

There is nothing cloak-and-dagger about the Federal Reserve. They issue pamphlets, magazines, monographs, and books that explain what central banking is all about. They conduct tours and provide speakers. They are delighted to discuss in detail why and how they did what they did one, two, or ten years ago. But the one thing they are reluctant to talk about, like central bankers throughout the world, is what they are doing today and what they are going to do tomorrow.

How, then, can we find out what some refer to as "our central bank" is up to? What kind of monetary policy is being featured this week—easy or tight, pinch or squeeze? Will it be held over next week by popular demand or replaced by a coming attraction?

To judge by the press, many financial observers rely on movements in the discount rate to indicate the current stance and future course of monetary policy. A change in the discount rate is headlined on the front page of the *New York Times* and solemnly announced in respectful tones by Walter Cronkite on the evening news. It is implied that when the Federal Reserve raises the discount rate, tight money is being ushered in, and when the discount rate is lowered, easy money is entering from the wings.

On the other hand, most Federal Reserve officials and academic economists agree that the discount rate is the *least* powerful of all the monetary instruments, too sluggish and lacking in punch to be a very sensitive barometer of monetary policy. So what indicators should we study? In order to assess the importance or unimportance of the discount rate and other indicators of central bank actions and intentions, let us first examine discount policy in some detail and then compare it with the other major tools of monetary policy—open-market operations and reserve requirements.

How Important Is the Discount Rate?

One of the primary functions of a central bank, perhaps *the* primary function, has always been to stand ready at all times to provide liquidity to the economy in case of financial stress or crisis. As the ultimate source of liquidity, the central bank is responsible for promptly supplying money on those rare but crucial occasions when the economy threatens to break down for lack of funds. For this reason, the central bank has traditionally been called the "lender of last resort" in emergency situations. In more ordinary circumstances, it also lends funds to banks that are temporarily short of reserves, as a means of smoothing out short-term variations in money-market conditions. When the central bank lends, for whatever purpose, the rate of interest it charges is called the discount rate.

The discount rate was considered the main instrument of central banking throughout the nineteenth century and for the first three decades of the twentieth. It reached its apogee in prestige in 1931, when England's Macmillan Committee, somewhat carried away by the splendor of it all, reported that the discount rate "is an absolute necessity for the sound management of a monetary system, and is a most delicate and beautiful instrument for the purpose."

The long tradition behind discounting and the corollary importance of the discount rate stem from the fact that until the mid-1920's it was virtually the only means available to the central bank to accomplish its purposes. Now, of course, with other instruments also at the Federal Reserve's disposal, the relative role of discounting has declined noticeably.

It should be mentioned at the outset that discount policy has two dimensions: one is *price*, the discount rate, the rate of interest the Federal Reserve charges commercial banks when they borrow from the Fed; the other is Federal Reserve surveillance over the *amount* that each bank is borrowing. Thus, one obvious flaw in using the discount rate alone as an indicator of monetary policy is that the rate might remain unchanged while the Federal Reserve employs more stringent (or more lenient) surveillance procedures. Monetary policy could thereby become tighter or easier, even through discount policy, but without any change in the discount rate.

The objective of raising the discount rate is just what the Federal Reserve says it is: to discourage commercial banks from borrowing at the Federal Reserve. When banks borrow from the Federal Reserve, their reserves increase and on that base they can expand their loans and investments and thereby the money supply. Less borrowing at the Federal Reserve because of a higher discount rate thus means less bank lending to business, a smaller growth in the money supply, and higher interest rates generally.

This process, it should be noted, provides no *direct* connection between changes in the discount rate and changes in market interest rates. The effects of a change in the discount rate are seen as operating through the mechanism of changes in bank reserves and the money supply, just as is the case with open-market operations and changes in reserve requirements. (However, as we point out in the next section, the magnitude of the effect on reserves of a change in the discount rate is minute, compared with the reserve effects of the two other tools available to the Federal Reserve.)

And yet, there does appear to be a direct connection between the discount rate and market interest rates. As can be seen in the following diagram, a close relationship exists between the discount rate and interest rates on short-term money-market instruments, such as treasury bills, and also between the discount rate and the prime bank lending rate, the interest rate banks charge their best business customers.

Careful examination, however, reveals that changes in treasury-bill yields typically *precede* changes in the discount rate. Treasury-bill yields rise, probably due to Federal Reserve open-market operations, and then—after they have risen quite a while and often quite a bit—the discount rate moves up. Or bill rates fall and then the discount rate is lowered. In other words, changes in the discount rate are likely to come *after* a basic switch in monetary policy has already occurred; they verify the switch and reinforce it, but they do not signal it.

On the other hand, a change in the discount rate often does precede a change in the prime rate because the posted prime rate is an administered rate that is changed relatively infrequently. Even here, however, changes in the standards banks set as to who qualifies for the prime rate will communicate the impact of open-market operations to bank borrowers before changes in the discount rate take place.

One possible way that changes in the discount rate might directly affect market interest rates is through the "announcement effect" produced when a discount-rate change comes unexpectedly. An unanticipated rise in the discount rate is likely to lead bondholders to expect tight money and higher interest rates (lower bond prices). They sell bonds to avoid capital losses, thus hastening the drop in bond prices and the rise in interest rates.

The key, of course, is that the rise in the discount rate under such circumstances generates expectations regarding future interest rates. But if the public had already observed tightening in the credit markets prior to the change in the discount rate, the actual announcement itself would produce very little reaction. In fact, the bond markets might be relieved of uncertainty, and interest rates might fall.

In any event, the bulk of the evidence suggests that while there may be some direct cause-and-effect connection between changes in the discount rate and changes in market interest rates, for the most part the relationship is indirect—through changes in bank reserves and the money supply. It also bears repeating that typically a change in the discount rate comes after, not before, a basic shift in monetary policy. It confirms what is going on but does not anticipate it. As an

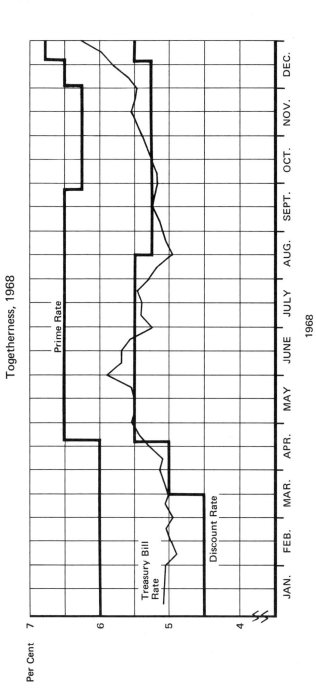

Togetherness, 1968

indicator, therefore, it is comparable to a fighter who learns his opponent's right cross is on the way when it crashes into his nose.

Discount Rate versus Reserve Requirements versus Open-Market Operations

If changes in the discount rate exert their main effects via bank reserves and the money supply, it is relevant to compare them in this respect with the other tools of monetary policy—changes in reserve requirements and open-market operations.

What proportion of member-bank reserves is attributable to the discounting process, to member banks' borrowing the reserves from the Federal Reserve? In 1950, total member-bank reserves were about $17 billion; less than half a billion of these reserves were acquired through the discount process. In 1969, member-bank reserves totaled about $27 billion; about $1 billion were due to borrowing from the Federal Reserve.

Over the entire twenty-year period of the 1950's and 1960's, borrowings from the Federal Reserve averaged about half a billion dollars annually. Even at its occasional peak levels of around $1.5 billion, discounting never provided as much as 10 per cent of total bank reserves and usually the percentage was much less—on average about 2 or 3 per cent.

The Federal Reserve does *not* use discount policy as a primary tool for changing bank reserves. For one thing, the initiative for discounting lies with the banks, not with the Federal Reserve. The Federal Reserve can lower the discount rate, but this does not force the banks to increase their borrowings. A change in the discount rate affects only those banks that are in debt to the Federal Reserve, or that consider such borrowing to be a likely source of funds. Many banks never borrow from the Federal Reserve except in dire emergency.

In addition, the Federal Reserve also views the "announcement effect" of discount-rate changes with mixed feelings. It might produce market behavior that is consistent with Federal Reserve objectives, as indicated above, but it cannot be relied upon and might do just the opposite. For example, if a rise in the discount rate leads borrowers to expect even tighter money in the future, they may hasten to borrow now, producing an increase in spending rather than a decrease.

Reserve-requirement changes, on the other hand, have an extremely powerful impact on bank-reserve positions and the money supply. A small change in the required reserve ratio instantly produces a rather large change in bank excess reserves. The April, 1969, increase of one-half of one percentage point in required reserves against demand deposits, for example, immediately shifted $650 million of reserves from the excess category, where they could have been used as a basis for loan and deposit expansion, to the required category, where for all practical purposes they were immobilized.

Because the impact is so powerful, so blunt, so immediate, and so widespread, the Federal Reserve uses its authority to change reserve requirements only sparingly. This reluctance is reinforced during tight money periods, when increases in reserve requirements would be appropriate. An increase in reserve requirements reduces commercial bank profitability, since banks then must hold a larger percentage of their assets in reserve balances that earn no interest. With membership in the Federal Reserve System voluntary (except for banks with national charters), the Federal Reserve is not anxious to discourage membership by raising reserve requirements too frequently. The "harsh hand of the Fed" is most evident when tight money is executed through higher reserve requirements. Since 1951, reserve requirements against demand deposits have been increased only five times and lowered on nine occasions. The discount rate, on the other hand, has been changed more than thirty times during the same period.

After all is said and done, the day-by-day standby of monetary policy, in good times and bad, is open-market operations. The purchase or sale of government securities can be undertaken in large or small amounts, as the Federal Reserve chooses. Tight or easy money can be initiated without announcement effects. The impact is fairly prompt, it is possible to proceed gradually, and to reverse field rapidly.

One reason market interest rates change before the discount rate changes is because the Federal Reserve has already been active with open-market operations. When the Federal Reserve alters the direction of monetary policy, it is typically open-market operations that lead the way. It is also open-market operations that do the brunt of the work as the new policy gathers momentum, with back-up support where necessary and appropriate from the discount rate and reserve requirements.

A Pride of Lions, a Gaggle of Geese, and a Plethora of Indicators

Unfortunately, since open-market operations are so unobtrusive, the search for reliable indicators of what the central bank is up to becomes more difficult than ever. The discount rate is generally not too helpful a guide to what the Federal Reserve is doing, except as confirmation of a change in monetary policy that has already occurred. A change in the direction of monetary policy can occur without any change in the discount rate, and conversely a change in the discount rate does not normally initiate a change in Federal Reserve policy.

Reserve-requirement changes are not of much assistance because they are used so seldom. Paradoxically, open-market operations are not very helpful for the opposite reason—they are used too frequently.

Weekly data on Federal Reserve open-market operations are released every Thursday afternoon and published in Friday's papers. But the knowledge that the Federal Reserve bought or sold so many government securities during any one week, or even over a succession of weeks, is in itself of limited value; the transactions may have been made simply to offset some "outside" factors that were affecting bank reserves, such as a seasonal inflow of currency, an outflow of gold to foreign countries, or any of a multitude of other possibilities.

Since it is widely understood that weekly data on open-market operations alone give an inadequate picture of what is going on, many financial observers rely heavily on movements in interest rates for clues to the current stance of monetary policy. Of all yields, the one most quickly responsive to monetary policy is probably the rate on short-term treasury bills.

However, as reliable indicators of what the central bank is doing, interest rates have serious limitations. To Monetarists, of course, as we saw in Chapter 5, they are irrelevant. Aside from that, it should be obvious that they are susceptible to change for reasons other than Federal Reserve policy; this makes it dangerous to read them as though they were determined exclusively by the Federal Reserve. The central bank has a substantial influence over the supply of credit, but only limited influence over the demand for it, so that interest rates may fluctuate for reasons that have nothing to do with the Federal Reserve's actions. Tight money generally means a rise in interest rates, but a rise in interest rates does not necessarily mean tight money.

Indeed, excessively *easy* money might also produce a rise in interest rates. A monetary policy that is too easy could generate inflationary expectations, thus leading lenders to withhold their funds from the market, unless they receive an interest rate that is sufficiently high to compensate them for receiving less valuable dollars when they are repaid their principal. If the going interest rate is 3 per cent, for example, and inflation then takes hold at the rate of 4 per cent a year, a lender who receives 7 per cent interest will still get only 3 per cent in terms of real purchasing power. Thus, interest rates could conceivably rise because of easy money as well as because of tight money.

Given the shortcomings of all the "orthodox" indicators—the discount rate, open-market transactions, and the behavior of interest rates—the Federal Reserve, always helpful, releases what it calls a Reserve Report each Thursday afternoon along with the data on open-market operations. The Reserve Report presents current statistics on a wide variety of alternative indicators. You can take your pick!

It lists weekly figures on all of the following: the monetary base, total member-bank reserves, the volume of member-bank discounting from the Federal Reserve, net free reserves, the money supply, the money supply plus time deposits, business loans at large commercial banks, and the bank credit proxy.

All these are self-explanatory except perhaps the monetary base, net free reserves, and the bank credit proxy. The monetary base is defined as total member-bank reserves plus currency outstanding. Net free reserves equals member-bank excess reserves less their borrowings from the Federal Reserve; when borrowings exceed excess reserves, it is usually called net borrowed reserves. The bank credit proxy is total deposits at member banks. It is employed as an early indicator of developing trends in bank credit, since data on deposits become available earlier than data on bank loans and investments.

With this smorgasbord of indicators, plus the orthodox ones that are on the back burner, you can select those that best suit your individual taste. As is obvious from Chapter 5, a Monetarist will lean toward the money supply in one form or another, a Keynesian toward interest rates, bank credit, and business loans. An eclectic will stuff himself on a little bit of everything, and if life becomes more complicated that way he has only himself to blame.

Free reserves attained some degree of popularity a few years ago but have recently fallen from favor. The main trouble is that a given level of free reserves is compatible with many different levels of the money supply and bank credit. The figure for free reserves has fluctuated within roughly the same limits for the past twenty years, while the money supply and bank credit have grown considerably during that interval.

The money supply has two derivative measures, the monetary base and total member-bank reserves. Both of these are closely related to the money supply and yet are somewhat more directly under the control of the Federal Reserve than the money supply itself. Each has as a weakness, however, that it includes borrowed reserves, which are not under the firm control of the Federal Reserve. Subtracting member-bank discounting from each of these probably provides the best measure of Federal Reserve actions with respect to the money supply. The *adjusted* monetary base or *un*borrowed reserves are thus favored by many Monetarists. If these increase, it implies that the Federal Reserve has engaged in open-market purchases and is trying to expand the money supply.

But even these are not unambiguous. It is quite true that if the adjusted monetary base or unborrowed reserves increases, we can be sure that the Federal Reserve is responsible for the change. We cannot be sure, however, that the Federal Reserve is trying to promote easier monetary conditions than it had been pursuing. Perhaps the demand for bank credit and money has increased. The monetary authorities may be trying to maintain the previous level of ease or restraint by meeting the increase in demand with an increase in supply. It is clear that an increase in the base is an expansionary move, but whether it signals a change from the previous level of ease or restraint is uncertain.

However, if we observe that as the monetary base expands, interest rates begin to fall, then the Federal Reserve has probably initiated a period of easier money. If interest rates remain unchanged when the monetary base increases, the central bank is most likely trying to maintain about the same degree of ease or tightness as before. But if interest rates go up when the base expands, then the Federal Reserve is sanctioning a somewhat tighter monetary policy, although not as tight as would have occurred if it had kept the monetary base stable.

It is evident that there simply is no reliable single all-purpose indicator of monetary policy. If all thirteen indicators we have mentioned give the same message, then there is no problem. But all too often some go off in one direction and some in another. And even with all those we have, not one is appropriate to measure, even roughly, such an important variable as changes in the degree of credit availability.

Obviously, if central banking is more art than science, as central bankers perennially avow, the same can be said thirteen-fold of deciphering what the central bankers are up to.

8

WHO'S IN CHARGE

HERE?

Monetary policy is the responsibility of the Federal Reserve, but to whom is the Federal Reserve responsible?

The answer to that question is so complex that if we successfully unravel it (which is a not too likely prospect), we possibly will have either unveiled one of the great socioeconomic creations in the annals of civilization, comparable to the invention of inside plumbing, or unmasked one of the most devious schemes ever contrived by the mind of man to camouflage the true locus of clandestine power.

According to some, the Federal Reserve is responsible to the Congress. But it is the president, not Congress, who appoints the members of the Board of Governors of the Federal Reserve System, the seven men (never yet a woman) who occupy the stately building at 20th Street and Constitution Avenue, Washington, D.C. The president also selects from among those seven the chairman of the Board of Governors, the principal spokesman for the central bank.

On that basis, one might surmise that the Federal Reserve is responsible to the executive branch of government, in the person of the president and his administration. However, since each member serves for a fourteen-year term, the current president can appoint only two of the seven-man Board of Governors, unless there are deaths or resignations. Even the chairman may be the appointee of the previous administration. Furthermore, it is Congress that created the Federal Reserve (not in its own image) in 1913, and it is Congress, not the president, that has the authority to alter its working mandate at any time. In 1935, for example, Congress chose to throw two administration representatives off the Board of Governors—namely, the secretary of the Treasury and the comptroller of the currency, both of whom had been ex officio members—simply because they were representatives of the executive branch.

Others, more cynical, have suggested that the Federal Reserve is mostly responsible to the private banking community, primarily the 6,000 commercial banks that are "member" banks of the Federal Reserve System. The member banks do in fact choose the presidents of each of the twelve regional Federal Reserve Banks, including the president of the most aristocratic one of all, the Federal Reserve Bank of New York. It may or may not be significant that the annual salary of the president of the Federal Reserve Bank of New York is $75,000, while that of the chairman of the Board of Governors in Washington is $42,500.

Who's in charge here? Who, indeed?

Formal Structure

The statutory organization of the Federal Reserve System is a case study in those currently popular concepts, decentralization and the blending of public and private authority. As the chart indicates, a deliberate attempt was made in the enabling congressional legislation to diffuse power over a broad base—geographically, between the private and public

The Formal Structure and Policy Organization of the Federal Reserve System

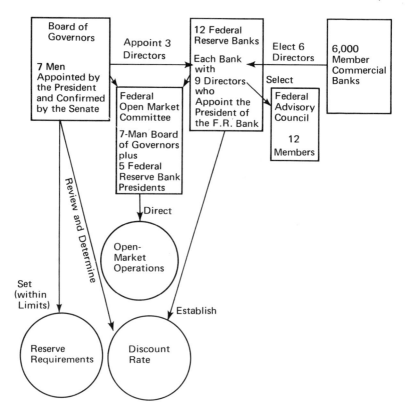

sectors, and even within the government—so that no one man, group, or sector, either inside or outside the government, can exert enough leverage to dominate the thrust of monetary policy.

The Board of Governors of the Federal Reserve System

consists of seven members, appointed by the president with the advice and consent of the Senate. In order to prevent presidential board-packing, each member is appointed for a term of fourteen years, with one term expiring at the end of January in each even-numbered year. Furthermore, no two board members may come from the same Federal Reserve district. The chairman of the Board of Governors is chosen from among the seven by the president and appointed for a four-year term. However, this term is not concurrent with the presidential term, so that an incoming president could find himself saddled with an already appointed chairman for most of his first term in office. The board is independent of the congressional appropriations process and of audit by the government's watchdog, the General Accounting Office, since its operating funds come from the earnings of the twelve regional Federal Reserve Banks.

The regional Federal Reserve Banks, one in each Federal Reserve district, are geographically dispersed throughout the nation—the Federal Reserve Bank of New York, the Federal Reserve Bank of Kansas City, the Federal Reserve Bank of San Francisco, and so on. Each Federal Reserve Bank is privately owned by the member banks in its district, the very commercial banks it is charged with supervising and regulating. However, the profits accruing to ownership are limited by law to a 6 per cent annual dividend on paid-in capital stock. The member bank stockholders elect six of the nine directors of their district Federal Reserve Bank, with the remaining three appointed from Washington by the Board of Governors. These nine directors, in turn, choose the president of their Federal Reserve Bank, subject to the approval of the Board of Governors.

The directors of each Federal Reserve Bank also select one person, always a commercial banker, to serve on the Federal

Advisory Council, a statutory body consisting of one member from each of the twelve Federal Reserve districts. The Federal Advisory Council consults quarterly with the Board of Governors in Washington and makes recommendations regarding the conduct of monetary policy.

Authority is similarly scattered in the execution of monetary policy in general, even with respect to the implementation of any single one of the instruments available to the central bank. The Board of Governors has the power to set reserve requirements on commercial bank time and demand deposits, for example, but it cannot set them outside the bounds of the specific and rather narrow limits imposed by the Congress (between 3 and 10 per cent for time deposits, between 7 and 14 per cent for demand deposits at smaller "country" banks, between 10 and 22 per cent for demand deposits at larger "city" banks).

Open-market operations are directed by a body known as the Federal Open Market Committee (FOMC), composed of the seven-man Board of Governors plus five of the Reserve Bank presidents. Since the members of the Board of Governors are appointed by the White House, and the Reserve Bank presidents are appointed by the directors of each Federal Reserve Bank, who are (six out of nine) elected by the member commercial banks, the diffusion of authority over even so important an instrument as open-market operations spans the distance from the White House to the member bank on Main Street. In addition, although the FOMC directs open-market operations, they are executed at the trading desk of the Federal Reserve Bank of New York by a gentleman who appears to be simultaneously an employee of the FOMC and the Federal Reserve Bank of New York.

Legal authority over discount rates is even more confusing. Discount rates are "established" every two weeks by the directors of each regional Federal Reserve Bank, but they are subject to "review and determination" by the Board of Governors. The distinction between "establishing" discount rates and "determining" them is a fine line indeed, and it would not be surprising if occasionally confusion arose as to precisely where the final authority and responsibility lie.

The Realities of Power

So much for the Land of Oz. In the real world, the facts of life are rather different, as the chart on page 85 indicates.

By all odds, the dominant figure in the formation and execution of monetary policy is the chairman of the Board of Governors of the Federal Reserve System. He is the most prominent member of the board itself, the most influential member of the FOMC; and generally recognized, by both Congress and the public at large, as *the* spokesman for the Federal Reserve System. Although the Federal Reserve Act appears to put all seven members of the Board of Governors on a more or less equal footing, over the past thirty-five years the strong personalities, outstanding abilities, and determined devotion to purpose of the chairmen—first Marriner S. Eccles and then William McChesney Martin—have made them rather more equal than the others. As adviser to the president, negotiator with Congress, and final authority on appointments throughout the system, with influence over all aspects of monetary policy in his capacity as chairman of both the Board of Governors and the FOMC, the chairman of the Board of Governors for all practical purposes is the embodiment of the central bank in this country.

The other six members of the Board of Governors also exercise a substantial amount of authority, more so than is indicated in the formal paper structure of the system, because with the passage of time primary responsibility for monetary policy has become more centralized and concentrated in Washington. When the Federal Reserve Act was first enacted, in 1913, it was thought that the Federal Reserve System would be mainly a passive service agency, supplying currency when needed, clearing checks, and providing a discount facility for the convenience of the private commercial member banks. At that time there was no conception of monetary policy as an active countercyclical force. Open-market operations were unknown and reserve requirements were fixed by law, with no flexibility permitted. Since then, of course, the central bank has shifted from passive accommodation to active regulation, from the performance of regional service functions to the implementation of national economic policy. This shift has been accompanied, naturally enough, by a rise in the power of the centralized Board of Governors and a corresponding decline in the role of the regional Federal Reserve Banks and their "owners," the commercial banks.

It would not be unrealistic to describe the central bank today as being headquartered in Washington, with twelve field offices located throughout the nation. These field offices may be known by the rather imposing name of Federal Reserve Banks, but they essentially amount to little more than branches of the Washington headquarters, nevertheless.

Closely related to the Board of Governors in the informal power structure, and deriving influence through that association, is the board's professional staff of economic experts and advisers. The long tenure in the Federal Reserve System of many senior staff economists, their familiarity with Federal Reserve history, and their expertise in monetary analysis give them a power base that is to a large extent founded on the respect with which they, as individuals, are held throughout the System. Through daily consultation with the individual governors and written and oral presentations before each

The Realities of Power within the Federal Reserve System

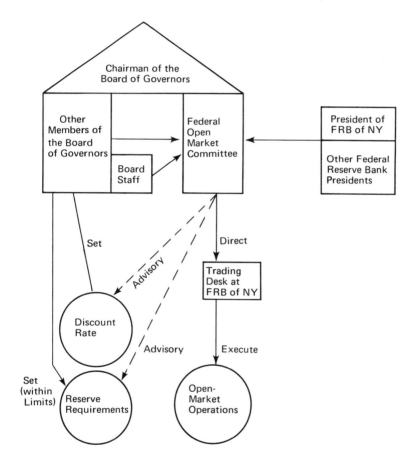

meeting of the FOMC, staff personnel exert an indefinable but significant influence on the ultimate decision-making process.

Aside from the Board of Governors, its chairman and its staff, the only other body playing a major role in Federal Reserve policy-making is the Federal Open Market Committee, which meets every three weeks in Washington. Out of the twelve members on the FOMC, a majority of seven are the Board of Governors members themselves. The other five, on a rotating basis, are Reserve Bank presidents. The president of the Federal Reserve Bank of New York is a permanent member of the FOMC, and the other eleven Federal Reserve Bank presidents alternate the remaining four seats among themselves.

The statutory authority of the FOMC is confined to the direction of open-market operations, but in recent years it has become the practice to bring all policy matters under review at the FOMC meetings. Although only five of the Reserve Bank presidents are entitled to vote at any one time, typically all twelve attend every meeting and participate in the discussion. Thus, potential reserve-requirement and discount-rate changes are, in effect, decided upon within the FOMC, with the twelve Reserve Bank presidents participating in an advisory capacity. The Board of Governors, however, always has the final say on reserve requirements and discount rates if matters should come to a showdown, particularly since legal opinion appears to be that in case of disagreement the board's power to "determine" discount rates overrides the authority of the individual Reserve Banks to "establish" them.

Once the Federal Open Market Committee decides on the appropriate open-market policy for the coming three-week interval, the actual execution of the policy directive until the next meeting is the responsibility of the account manager at the Federal Reserve Bank of New York's trading desk. Since the FOMC's instructions are generally couched in rather broad language—to conduct open-market operations so as to attain "somewhat easier conditions" in the money market, or so as to "move toward firmer conditions"—the account manager has to translate these vague instructions into actual daily purchases and sales of treasury securities. In the process, at least a modest amount of leeway and personal interpretation is inevitable. Like the account manager, the unique position of the president of the Federal Reserve Bank of New York in the hierarchy also stems from his role and status in the nation's financial center. If he is inclined to use this leverage, as Allan Sproul did a decade or two ago and Benjamin Strong before him, the president of the New York Reserve Bank can mount a substantial challenge even to the chairman of the Board of Governors. Since such a challenge would have little legal foundation, it would have to be based on the prestige of the presidency of the Federal Reserve Bank of New York and the forcefulness of the man who holds the position. Both Sproul and Strong were men of exceptional ability and personality.

But where, in the corridors of power, does this leave the member banks, the directors of each Federal Reserve Bank, and the Federal Advisory Council? Pretty much shut out, if the truth be known.

The member banks do indeed "own" their district Federal Reserve Bank, but such stockholding is mostly symbolic and carries with it none of the usual attributes of ownership. The member banks also have a major voice in electing the directors of their Reserve Bank, but the directors in turn have responsibilities that are largely ceremonial. True, they appoint the members of the Federal Advisory Council, but the Federal Advisory Council serves mostly a public relations purpose and has little to do with policy-making. The directors of each Federal Reserve Bank also choose the president of their Reserve Bank, subject to the approval of the Board of Governors.

But the "subject to approval" clause has meant, in practice, that the most the directors can really do is submit a list of nominees for the position. On more than one occasion, the choice of the directors of a Federal Reserve Bank has not met with approval from Washington; in such cases, it has become very clear exactly where ultimate authority is lodged.

How Independent the Central Bank?

The fact that ultimate authority over monetary policy resides in Washington brings to the fore the relationship between the central bank and the other branches of government also responsible for overall national economic policy—the Congress and the administration, the latter personified by the president.

The Federal Reserve is a creature of the Congress. The Constitution gives Congress the power "to coin money and regulate the value thereof." On this basis, Congress created the Federal Reserve System as the institution delegated to administer that responsibility on its behalf. Congress requires periodic accountability by the Federal Reserve and has the power to alter or amend the enabling legislation, the Federal Reserve Act, any time it sees fit.

Essentially, Congress has given the Federal Reserve a broad mandate to regulate the monetary system in the public interest and then, more or less, has stood aside and let the monetary authorities pursue this objective on their own and to the best of their abilities. Congress has also attempted to minimize interference on the part of the administration by giving each member of the Board of Governors a fourteen-year term, thereby sharply limiting any one president's influence over the board.

This semi-independent status of the central bank is a source of continuous friction. A small minority of Congress appears to believe that the Federal Reserve has carried its "independence" much too far. There has been some concern over its freedom from congressional appropriations and from standard government audit. Also, the Federal Reserve's responsibility on occasion for tight money and high interest rates has, from time to time, stimulated intensive questioning at congressional hearings, including frequent scoldings of Federal Reserve officials by Populist-minded congressmen who get uptight about tight money.

Others, in Congress and out, have complained that the Federal Reserve simply has not done a very good job, that we would all be better off if Congress laid down some guidelines or rules to limit the discretion available to the monetary authorities in conducting their business. We will discuss such proposals further in Chapter 17.

The relationship between the central bank and the president has also aroused considerable controversy. Many feel that the Federal Reserve should be a part of the administration, responsible to the president, on the grounds that monetary policy is an integral part of national economic policy. Monetary policy should therefore be coordinated at the highest level (that is, by the president), along with fiscal policy, as a component part of the administration's total program for economic growth and stability.

To do otherwise, it is charged, is both undemocratic and divisive. Undemocratic, because monetary policy is too important to be run by an elite group of experts insulated from the political process. Divisive, because monetary and fiscal policy should not work at cross-purposes. Since fiscal policy proposals are clearly within the president's domain, monetary policy should be as well. A Federal Reserve independent of presidential authority conflicts with the administration's responsibility to promulgate and coordinate an overall economic program.

On the other hand, the case for central bank independence from the executive branch of government rests on the pragmatic basis that subordination of the central bank to the executive invites excessive money creation and consequent inflation. The charge that an independent Federal Reserve is undemocratic is countered by the reminder that the central bank is still very much responsible to Congress. In addition, the chairman of the Board of Governors confers regularly with the president, the secretary of the Treasury, and the chairman of the president's Council of Economic Advisers.

It is feared by many, and not without historical justification, that if the monetary authority is made the junior partner to the president or the Treasury (the fiscal authority), monetary stability will be sacrificed to the government's revenue needs—that the government will be tempted to seek the easy way out in raising funds, by printing money or borrowing excessively at artificially low interest rates, in preference to the politically more difficult route of raising taxes or cutting back on government spending. The sole purpose of an independent monetary authority, in brief, is to forestall the asserted natural propensity of governments to resort to inflation.

PART II

Specific Issues

9

ARE HIGH

INTEREST RATES

ALWAYS BAD?

It is time for a pop quiz. Compare yourself with the experts. Check all those you know, way down deep, are more true than false:

High interest rates
( ) result from collusion between Wall Street and Big Business.
( ) make the rich richer and the poor poorer.
( ) create unemployment and cause depression.
( ) raise prices and cause inflation.

We all think we know the answers. But do we? Have we ever really thought them through? The time has come to put the cards on the table.

The Conspiratorial Interpretation of Interest Rates

There is a deep-seated suspicion in American society that conspiracy is everywhere afoot. Television programs are awful because "they" want them that way. Stocks go up or down because "insiders" are rigging the market. Rents are high because the landlords are ganging up on the rest of us. The Yankees always won because that's how "they" wanted it; now "they" don't want it that way any more, so the Yankees lose. The Establishment thinks the campus disruptions are manipulated by a few hard-core conspirators (two SDS members, a Black Panther, a Soviet attaché, and a professor); and the militants think the military-industrial complex (in the person of a general, two corporation presidents, a United States senator, and a professor) is plotting behind closed doors to manipulate everybody else. We've all seen too many Westerns. So why should interest rates be any different?

Insofar as interest rates are concerned, and regardless of the merits of these other matters (although the only one that sounds plausible to us is the one concerning the Yankees), it is in fact extremely doubtful that any one individual or group in the United States, aside from the Federal Reserve and perhaps the United States Treasury, has anywhere near enough power even to influence interest rates much less set them.

That statement may be a slight exaggeration. But even if it is, it is still much closer to reality than the more popular conspiratoral theory of interest-rate determination. For the simple reason that in this country there are too many lenders engaged in the business of lending, and therefore too many alternatives open to most would-be borrowers, to make it possible for any tightly knit clique of lenders (or borrowers, for that matter) to control the price of credit. They would love to. Who doubts that? But they are not *able* to. The wish, as 93-year-old George Bernard Shaw commented when he considered marrying Brigitte Bardot, is not always father to the deed.

Suppose that the three largest banks in the United States —the Bank of America, Chase Manhattan, and the First National City Bank of New York, with aggregate assets amounting to $60 billion (out of total bank assets of $500 billion)—were to decide, in concert, to raise interest rates above prevailing levels during a time when there was *no overall upward pressure on rates.* Could they pull it off?

Not very likely. Quite aside from the anti-trust laws, their business customers would simply shift to other banks, or decide to raise their funds in the commercial paper market, or float bonds in the nationwide corporate bond market, or utilize any one of a wide variety of other potential alternatives. Consumers could also shift to another bank, or to a savings and loan association, or to their local credit union. If the three would-be monopolists wanted to continue doing very much business, they would have little choice but to bring their rates back into line.

Even the Federal Reserve does not have enough power to set interest rates at whatever level it pleases, whenever it wishes. The central bank may control the supply of credit, but it does not control the demand, and both are involved in the determination of its price. In the immediate postwar years, the Federal Reserve, under pressure from the United States Treasury, decided to try to hold interest rates at low prewar depression levels. It succeeded, but in the process lost control over the supply of money and helped fuel the inflation then erupting.

The facts of life, in this case at least, are rather prosaic. There is considerable competition in the market for loanable funds: competition among lenders for potential credit-worthy borrowers and competition among borrowers for the available supply of funds. Lenders charging more than prevailing rates will price themselves out of the market and lose business to their competitors. Borrowers trying to borrow at cheaper rates will find themselves outbid for funds by others.

The Rich Get Richer and the Poor Get Poorer

Inequality in the distribution of income may possibly be getting worse. However, there is some hopeful evidence to the contrary in a few countries, including the United States, Great Britain, Scandinavia, and Castro's Cuba. But whatever the facts, the fault hardly lies with the interest rate, high or low.

The blame for continued bedrock poverty in the United States might conceivably be attributed to capitalism, but if so—and the evidence is less than convincing—it has little to do with the interest rate. Socialist and communist economies have interest rates as well as capitalist ones. Indeed, regardless of the type of economic system, wherever funds are scarce and have alternative immediate as well as future uses there will be interest rates, whatever they are called.

It deserves mention, by the way, that financial institutions *pay out* interest as well as take it in. Currently the largest category of bank costs is interest paid out to depositors, a larger cost item than even wages and salaries. Assuming that all bankers are rich and all depositors poor, an unlikely assumption if there ever was one, the flow of interest on savings deposits—which increases when interest rates rise—redistributes income from the rich to the poor. The financial position of small depositors and bondholders is often ignored when the income-redistribution effects of high interest rates are discussed.

The fact of the matter is that the causes of poverty in this country have little to do with interest rates. The primary reasons for most of our poverty are much less complicated than the intricacies of money, financial markets, or fluctuations in interest rates. The poor get poorer because to a large extent they are elderly or unskilled or black or Puerto Rican or Mexican-American or Indian. They get poorer because they are elderly and inflation erodes their savings, or because they are unskilled and unable to compete in the job market, or because the skills they do possess have been made obsolete by the onrush of technology.

For many, poverty is quite simply the bitter legacy of several centuries of sharp-edged bigotry; the fruit of persistent, widespread, and systematic prejudice against racial, religious, and nationality minorities in education, housing, and employment. They get poorer not because interest rates are high but because they get third-rate educations in inferior schools; because they are denied access to clean and decent housing; because they encounter a mountainous avalanche of employer discrimination in job advancement and union discrimination in admission and apprentice requirements; because they are tangled up in a topsy-turvy welfare system that penalizes initiative, discourages family ties, and fosters dependency and cynicism.

For the most part, high interest rates are a contrived scapegoat. The elimination of hard-core poverty does not lie in perpetually low interest rates. It lies in an overhaul of our educational system, in adequate job-training programs, in more sensible welfare and social security arrangements, and in the maintenance of a high-employment economy without inflation within which there is full and complete equality of opportunity for everyone.

Do High Interest Rates Create Unemployment?

Tight money and the high interest rates it typically induces
are not designed to create unemployment. Tight money is
intended to prevent inflation or at least slow it down. However, some object strenuously to its use as an anti-inflationary weapon on the grounds that it is a very dangerous
instrument which cannot be used in moderation—that if
effective at all, it is likely to be *too effective,* setting off a
financial crisis and an ensuing recession.

Thus, Alvin Hansen, for years the foremost American
Keynesian, wrote in 1949:

> The monetary weapon has the peculiar characteristic that
> it is scarcely at all effective unless the brakes are applied so
> vigorously as to precipitate a collapse. Those who glibly talk
> about controlling inflation by monetary policy have failed to
> consider that moderate monetary measures by themselves alone
> are relatively ineffective, while drastic measures may easily turn
> the economy into a tailspin.

A decade later, in 1959, in a report for the Joint Economic
Committee of the Congress, practically the same thesis was
reasserted by Warren Smith, who several years later was to
become a member of President Johnson's Council of Economic Advisers: "It is perhaps just as well that monetary
controls have not been very effective; if they had been, they
might have been disastrous."

And right on schedule, ten years after *that,* in 1969, the
same views were put forth by others, particularly the trade
unions, as soon as monetary policy began to tighten in the
early months of the year.

Assessments of monetary policy along these lines are paralyzing. If taken seriously, monetary policy would be employed so gingerly in fighting inflation that it could hardly be anything but useless. We have now had, in the postwar period, approximately two decades of more-or-less active countercyclical monetary policy, sometimes devoted to offsetting recession and sometimes to counteracting inflation. And thus far, tight money, periodically imposed, has not precipitated either Hansen's tailspin or Smith's disaster.

Every economic policy involves some degree of risk. The Federal Reserve might indeed go too far. But on the basis of the record up to now, the potential depression risk involved in actively employing tight money to check inflation appears to be far less than the potential inflation risk of being afraid to ever use monetary policy at all.

In the years before World War II, mass unemployment was the dominant economic problem in this country. In the broad sweep of the postwar period, the major concern has not been depression, but inflation. It will not be possible to effectively fight the economic problems of the 1970's, whatever they may be, if we continue to think only in terms of the problems of the 1930's.

Do High Interest Rates Make Inflation Worse?

Although the announced purpose of tight money is to restrain inflation, complaints against its use have consistently come from critics who believe that high interest rates make inflation *worse* rather than better. Since interest is one of the costs of doing business, it is argued, higher interest rates, like higher wages, tend to *raise* rather than lower prices.

Congressman Wright Patman of Texas is a leading proponent of this point of view, as are spokesmen for organized labor. Surprisingly, there is possibly more truth in this position than in any of the others discussed in this chapter, and it may contain more validity than most professional economists—who refuse to take it seriously and typically dismiss it out of hand—are willing to admit.

Higher interest rates *do* increase costs, and thereby push prices up from the supply side. They also *do* result in larger incomes for lenders, owners of savings deposits, and bondholders, enabling them to increase their spending, thereby pulling prices up from the demand side. Cost push and demand pull. On the surface, at least, higher interest rates are not so different from higher wage rates. If the latter are inflationary, why not the former?

The standard response to these arguments is that interest is so small an element of business costs, and of income, that higher rates don't matter that much. But such a response raises more questions than it answers. Indeed, it goes so far that it all but destroys the orthodox case for higher interest rates made by the proponents of monetary policy themselves—which is that higher rates lower investment spending, decrease aggregate demand, and thus reduce inflationary pressures. If interest is so minute an element of business costs, then how can higher rates be expected to significantly affect investment spending, as the proponents of monetary policy claim?

The fact is that interest is *not* a negligible item in business costs. In expenditures for long-lived plant or equipment, particularly, it may be a crucial component of costs. For example, if you buy a $20,000 home and get a mortgage for the full amount at 7 per cent interest for thirty years, before all is over and done with, you will be paying $28,000 in interest and the $20,000 house will wind up costing you

$48,000. If the interest rate increases to 8 per cent, your total interest payments will add up to $33,000 and the house will cost you $53,000, almost triple its list price.

Furthermore, interest is no trivial component of national income. In recent years it has been running at about 10 per cent of personal after-tax income.

The orthodox response, then, to the "higher interest rates raise prices" argument is wrong. If that were the only answer, the heretics would be far more correct than the traditionalists, even on the traditionalists' own grounds. The answer, if there is any, will have to be found elsewhere.

Yet surely there *must* be an answer. If not, tight money to stop inflation has been exceedingly harmful. It has made the inflation of the past twenty years even worse than it would otherwise have been. If that is so, what *is* appropriate monetary policy when inflation threatens? Should we have *easy* money? Should we try to *lower* interest rates?

The answer to the "high interest rates raise prices" school of thought lies in a closer examination of the assumed similarity between the effects of higher wage rates and the effects of higher interest rates. In Chapter 4 we pointed out that higher wage rates are inflationary. Wage increases in excess of productivity gains mean higher costs, thereby putting upward cost pressure on prices from the supply side. Higher wages also mean larger incomes for wage-earners, thereby generating an increase in consumer spending which pulls prices up from the demand side. Congressman Patman and others claim that higher interest rates do exactly the same thing. *And Congressman Patman is right.* Higher interest rates *do* raise costs and incomes, and *do* thereby generate cost-push and demand-pull inflationary pressures. To deny this by claiming that interest is an insignificant component of costs or of income is simply wrong. It is also about as damaging to the rationale for orthodox monetary policy as the congressman's views.

In Chapter 4 we also pointed out, however, that wage increases, *alone,* could not fully explain either cost-push or demand-pull inflation. To maintain inflation for any sustained period of time, wage increases must be accompanied by two other conditions: market power in the hands of Big Business and, most important of all, a full employment guarantee underwritten by Big Government. Without the support of the Employment Act, neither Big Labor nor Big Business, individually or in concert, could continue a wage-price spiral for very long.

Monetary policy, of course, is one of the primary instruments used to implement the Employment Act. If every time labor won a large wage increase, and businessmen jacked up prices correspondingly, the central bank increased the money supply to bail them out, inflation would proceed virtually without interruption. Such increases in the money supply are a necessary condition for the continuation of rising prices over the long run. But if the central bank does *not* increase the money supply, or actually reduces it, inflation will sooner or later peter out, regardless of the strength of unions or the monopoly power of business.

The crucial difference between wage increases in excess of productivity gains and interest rate increases that result from tight money lies precisely here. Excessive wage increases accompanied by injections of new money are indeed inflationary. So would be higher interest rates accompanied by injections of new money. However, wage increases that are not accompanied by additions to the money supply, or that are followed by actual reductions in the stock of money, will result in a rising price level for only a short while. In effect, the full employment guarantee will have been cancelled and, without fuel, inflation will soon run its course.

The rising interest rates that result from tight money should be compared *not* with higher wages plus an enlarged money supply, which is typically the comparison that is implicitly made, but with higher wage rates accompanied by a constant or lower money supply—as if every time wages increased by so many per cent, the central bank automatically cut back the rate of growth in the money supply a similar per cent. For this, in general terms, is what happens when interest rates rise during a period of tight money.

Such higher interest rates, like higher wages under similar circumstances, may raise the price level briefly, but if the central bank sticks to its guns it will not go up far or for long. With a constant or lower money supply, further increases in the price level would be difficult to finance, the higher interest rates will choke off some spending, and sooner or later total expenditures will stop rising. At that point the inflation process will grind to a halt.

10

WHAT IS FINANCIAL

INTERMEDIATION?

Financial intermediation played an important role, it is said, in permitting monetary velocity to rise during the 1950's. Financial *dis*intermediation, on the other hand, was a significant factor in aggravating the intense credit crunch of 1966. The words are big, but the process, it turns out, is familiar. Add to those who have been talking prose all their lives and were not aware of it, the millions who have been engaged in some aspect of financial intermediation or disintermediation and did not realize it.

Financial intermediaries are nothing more than financial institutions—such as commercial and savings banks, savings and loan associations, credit unions, pension funds, insurance companies, and the like—that act as middlemen, transferring funds from original savers (or ultimate lenders) on one side of the counter to ultimate borrowers on the other. They borrow from Peter in order to lend to Paul. What all of them have in common is that they acquire funds by issuing their own liabilities to the public (savings deposits, savings and loan shares) and then they turn around and use this money to buy financial assets (stocks, bonds, mortgages) for themselves.

Because these institutions exist, savers who do not want to hoard their cash under a mattress, but who feel hesitant about purchasing corporate bonds or stocks or mortgages because they feel that these assets are perhaps too risky or too illiquid, are given a third alternative: They can "purchase" savings deposits or savings and loan shares. In that way, they can hold a relatively safe and quite liquid financial asset, yet still earn *some* interest income. Nevertheless, the corporations and potential home-owners can still sell their bonds, stocks, and mortgages—to the financial intermediaries rather than to the original savers themselves. Financial intermediaries, in brief, "intermediate" between original savers, on the one hand, and final borrowers, on the other.

Financial intermediation is precisely the above process: savers depositing funds with financial institutions, rather than directly buying bonds or mortgages, with the financial institutions, in turn, doing the lending to the ultimate borrowers. Disintermediation is the reverse: savers taking funds out of deposit accounts, or reducing the amounts they normally put in, and investing directly, in their own name, in market securities such as stocks and bonds.

Financial Intermediation Lowers Interest Rates

As a general proposition, interest rates on securities (bonds, stocks, mortgages, and so forth) exist in order to induce the public to bear the risks inherent in owning them—risks such as potential capital losses due to interest-rate fluctuations, possible default, illiquidity, and so on. In other words, the borrower must pay the lender for parting with the most liquid of all assets, money, and holding in its place a relatively illiquid security.

Financial institutions are in a better position than individuals to bear and spread the risks of security ownership. Because of their large size, intermediaries can diversify their portfolios and minimize the risk involved in holding any one security. They are experts in evaluating borrower credit characteristics. They employ skilled portfolio managers and can take advantage of administrative economies in large-scale buying and selling.

For these reasons, they can afford to receive lower yields on their assets and will accept them if they have to. Competition among financial intermediaries forces interest rates to the lowest level that is compatible with their evaluation of the risks of security ownership. These yields are lower than if the same securities were held by individual investors, unable to minimize their risks so efficiently.

Looked at in another way, financial institutions also help to reduce the demand for money, thereby contributing to lower interest rates. People hold money both for day-to-day transactions and also for safety, due to the riskiness of stock or bond holding (relative to cash). But such intermediary liabilities as savings deposits and savings and loan shares are also safe, as safe as money, and virtually as liquid. Indeed, they are so safe and liquid that they are often called near-monies or money substitutes.

With such safe and liquid assets available—ones that earn interest to boot—people will have less desire to hold money itself. They can be almost as liquid (and also earn some interest) if they substitute savings deposits in place of some of their cash holdings. The money that people release and deposit in financial intermediaries will be used, in turn, by the intermediaries to buy bonds, mortgages, and so on. Thus additional money enters the bond market and bond prices are bid up (interest rates drop). The net effect of financial intermediation is to lower interest rates.

There are many ways of looking at this process. We have just seen that the demand for bonds goes up: With a given supply of bonds, this drives bond prices up. Alternatively, we have also seen that the demand for money falls: Since the supply of money remains unchanged (it is determined by the Federal Reserve, not by the public), this means that the supply of money is now greater than the demand, which tends to lower interest rates. Still another indication of inter-mediation is revealed by the behavior of velocity: Spending on goods and services can be increased when intermediary liabilities rise, as formerly idle cash is made available to finance ultimate borrowers. And when GNP goes up while the money supply does not, an increase in velocity results.

The growth in financial intermediaries has been spec-tacular in the last twenty-five years. Savings deposits in commercial banks have grown from $30 billion at the end of World War II to over $200 billion, and savings and loan shares have increased from less than $10 billion to over $130 billion. At the same time, we have experienced a general *increase* in the level of interest rates. This does not neces-sarily contradict what we have said above. If all other factors had remained the same, the growth in intermediation should have reduced interest rates. But, of course, all other factors have not remained the same.

Both the money supply and intermediary liabilities have been growing, providing us with increased liquidity. How-ever, this has been more than absorbed both by the sustained growth in the demand for funds by ultimate borrowers, floating more and more new bonds; and by the rise in GNP and the price level, both of which have increased the demand for cash for transactions purposes. The net effect has been that the increase in the demand for liquidity has outpaced the increase in the supply of liquidity, so that interest rates have risen. In light of the volume of borrowing and the rise in prices and GNP since World War II, what is surprising, and must be attributed in large part to the growth of intermediation, is that the rise in interest rates has not been considerably greater.

It is worth noting that since financial intermediation tends to lower interest rates, or at least moderate any increase, it has been highly beneficial to our rate of economic growth. A high rate of economic growth requires a heavy volume of real investment. The lower the rate of interest that ultimate borrowers must pay, the greater their expenditure on real investment is likely to be.

The beneficial effect of intermediation on economic growth can also be seen from the viewpoint of risk-bearing. Intermediaries are better able than individuals to bear the risks of lending out venture capital. As was previously stressed, ability to diversify, economies of scale, and expertise in lending account for this comparative advantage of institutions over individuals. As financial intermediaries own a larger and larger portion of the marketable securities outstanding, the subjective risk borne by the economy is lowered, interest rates are reduced, and more real investment takes place. Funds are channeled from ultimate lenders, through intermediaries, to ultimate borrowers more efficiently than if the intermediaries did not exist.

Intermediation and Monetary Policy

One of the most widely debated contributions to monetary theory and policy in recent years has come to be known as the "Gurley-Shaw Thesis," after its originators and chief expositors, John Gurley and Edward Shaw, both of Stanford University.

Gurley and Shaw emphasize that the deposit liabilities of savings and loan associations, savings banks, and other financial intermediaries are, after all, not much different from the demand-deposit liabilities of commercial banks, even though we call only the latter money. It is true that we can spend demand deposits, and that we cannot spend a savings and loan share, at least not without cashing it in first. But cashing it in is a simple matter, easily accomplished; thus savings and loan shares and savings deposits, whether at commercial banks or at savings banks, are for all practical purposes almost as liquid as demand deposits.

Gurley and Shaw conclude that since these near-monies are outside the jurisdiction of the Federal Reserve, they make the successful execution of monetary policy difficult. Controlling liquidity only through the money supply will not work very well, since liquidity can also be provided by near-monies. Similarly, controlling the lending of commercial banks, which the Federal Reserve can do, will not accomplish much if the lending of all other financial intermediaries, over which the Federal Reserve has no direct control, is left unhampered.

According to Gurley and Shaw, the problem is especially acute in the case of anti-inflationary monetary policy. Assume the Federal Reserve reduces the money supply in order to inhibit spending on real and financial assets. Interest rates on market securities rise. Now the intermediaries go into action. Aware of the higher yields and the profits they imply, savings banks raise the rate they offer on deposits in an effort to attract more funds, funds they can then invest in the higher-yielding securities. The increase in deposit rates induces some individuals to put more funds in savings banks, savings and loan associations, and the like. Financial intermediation is in full swing.

The individuals shifting money to the intermediaries may use funds they formerly had directly invested in securities, thus rebuilding their liquidity; and they may use what were idle money balances, now coaxed out of hiding by the attractive rates posted and widely advertised by the intermediaries. As long as the latter occurs to some extent, there will be a net expansion in the demand for market securities (by the intermediaries), a consequent moderation in the rise in interest rates, and—most important of all—the channeling of previously idle money balances into the eager hands of ultimate borrower-spenders.

With spending unchecked and the money supply curtailed, velocity will rise and everyone will say the Federal Reserve can't stop inflation because it can't control velocity. But Gurley and Shaw would say the Federal Reserve can't stop inflation because it can't control financial intermediation and the creation of near-monies.

The Gurley-Shaw hypothesis, which was first developed in the mid-1950's here and at about the same time in England by the Radcliffe Committee, appeared to be vindicated by the experience of the 1950's and early 1960's. At that time, tight money invariably was accompanied by the mobilization of idle balances, an expansion in intermediation, and consequent financing of the boom by the intermediaries. Debate raged as to whether the Federal Reserve should have the power to set reserve requirements for savings banks and savings and loan associations, and congressional hearings were held to explore ways to solve the problem.

But perhaps the problem solved itself, or was solved accidentally. Because the Great Credit Squeeze of 1966 was a different story.

Disintermediation

During the tight money episode of 1966, market interest rates rose to what were then record levels, but the expected financial intermediation did not take place. Deposit rates did not go up as rapidly as open-market rates on securities—and savers, instead of shifting funds *to* financial intermediaries, shifted them *out*. Individuals removed funds from savings accounts and put the money directly into corporate, municipal, and government securities. Financial disintermediation had occurred, the opposite of what we had been having for twenty years!

This put the intermediaries under severe pressure. With substantial withdrawals and minimal inflows of new funds, their profit position was threatened, their solvency was endangered, and their ability to lend to ultimate borrowers evaporated. They reacted as financial institutions will—by pulling in their horns, trying to retrench, and running to Congress for help. In other words, they aggravated tight money conditions instead of, as before, ameliorating them.

What happened?

Market rates went so high so fast that the intermediaries, for both internal and external reasons, could not raise the rates they pay depositors high enough or fast enough to stay competitive. Disappointed, depositors drowned their sorrow by going out and buying the high-yielding securities on their own.

Two reasons prevented the intermediaries from sufficiently adjusting their deposit rates to stay competitive with open-market rates. Internally, they felt they could not afford to. The assets of most intermediaries are primarily long-term in nature; most were bought some time ago, at considerably lower yields. The average rate of return is thus heavily weighted by the past. The purchase of new, higher-yielding securities will only slightly increase the overall yield on the total portfolio.

On the other hand, if they increase their deposit rates to attract new money, they have no choice but to pay the new higher rates to *all* depositors.

In 1966, market rates moved up so far and so rapidly that most financial institutions felt, after a brief attempt to stay in the race, that it was too costly to continue. They had, to put it bluntly, been priced out of the market.

But there was another reason why they did not stay in the race, an external one. Some intermediaries—perhaps the better managed ones—were all for posting higher deposit rates and going after new business. But they couldn't. The legal rate ceilings, imposed by the Federal Reserve, the Federal Home Loan Bank Board, and other supervisory agencies, prevented them from raising deposit rates further once the maximum limits had been reached.

Indeed, in mid-1966 the deposit-rate ceilings were actually rolled back to lower levels, forcing many institutions that had posted higher interest rates to reduce them. With market rates still rising, it is no wonder depositors withdrew their money and went directly into the securities markets.

Deposit-Rate Ceilings

The Federal Reserve sets the legal maximum interest rates—through what is known as Regulation Q—that commercial banks are allowed to pay on their time and savings deposit liabilities. (The savings departments of commercial banks, as contrasted with their demand deposit business, are usually considered financial intermediaries similar to savings banks or savings and loan associations.) The maximum interest rates that the savings banks and savings and loan associations may offer depositors are also regulated. If these ceilings are set above going deposit rates, they are inoperative and irrelevant. But once deposit rates push up against the ceilings, they tend effectively to inhibit intermediation by preventing financial institutions from competing against open-market securities for funds. To the extent that disintermediation results, open-market rates will rise even higher than otherwise.

For this reason, when we are in a period of tight money and the regulatory authorities fail to raise Regulation Q and the comparable regulations over the other intermediaries (or actually lower the ceilings, as they did in 1966) they are making monetary policy even more restrictive. When Regulation Q and its counterparts are raised, as was always done prior to 1966, this is viewed as an easing sign.

This may seem a bit peculiar—considering the lowering of an interest rate to be a sign of tightness, the raising of a rate a sign of ease. Once the intermediation process is recognized, however, it is clear that a lowering of Q induces financial disintermediation, and thereby higher market interest rates; while an increase in Q promotes financial intermediation, and thereby lower market interest rates, especially long-term rates.

An increase in Q tends to make bank time deposits more attractive than competing, highly liquid, short-term financial instruments, such as treasury bills. This may raise short-term interest rates on treasury bills, as people and corporations shift from bills to deposits. But as the intermediaries, in turn, buy long-term financial assets with the funds, long rates tend to fall. Since investment spending is related primarily to long-term rates rather than short rates, the entire process is expansionary.

Regulation Q has thus turned out to be one of the most powerful instruments the Federal Reserve possesses, with profound and pervasive effects comparable even to open-market operations. When it was passed in 1913, the Federal Reserve Act contained no provision of any sort fixing maximum permissible interest rates that banks could pay on their time and savings deposits. At that time, this was not considered an appropriate area of regulation. Twenty years later, in 1933, Congress instructed the Federal Reserve to set such rate ceilings on commercial banks. However, the ceilings were always raised to higher levels whenever they became troublesome—until 1966. At that time, similar rate ceilings were imposed on competing deposit-type financial institutions and, instead of being raised, they were lowered. Since then, the lid has been kept on firmly and tightly.

The 1933 provision was enacted on the grounds that excessive interest-rate competition for deposits during the 1920's had undermined the soundness of the banking system. It was believed that competition among banks had driven deposit rates up too high, resulting in such high bank costs that the banks, in turn, were led to acquire high-yielding but excessively risky low-quality assets, thereby contributing to the collapse of the banking system in the early 1930's. Similar arguments were responsible for the imposition of comparable ceilings over other intermediaries starting in 1966.

This analysis is open to serious question. In retrospect, it is not at all clear that the historical experience on which Regulation Q was based was correctly interpreted at the time the legislation was enacted. Interest rates on bank time and

"Just because you and I don't like the interest-rate ceilings, we don't go storming the Treasury Building, do we?"

Drawing by Wm. Hamilton;
© 1968 by The New Yorker Magazine, Inc.

savings deposits actually declined during the 1920's, and thorough investigation since has failed to substantiate any appreciable deterioration in the quality of bank assets during that period.

With respect to the early 1930's, what was once interpreted as a banking collapse due to mismanagement by commercial bankers now appears to be much more a case of

banking collapse due to inadequate *central* banking. There is
rather widespread agreement today that, had the Federal
Reserve stepped in promptly and vigorously, the greater part
of the banking debacle of the early 1930's could have been
avoided.

But whether Regulation Q is based on a premise that is
true or false—and one which in any case had very little to do
with financial intermediation—no longer appears to matter
very much. From all indications, it will probably be with us,
for better or worse, for a very long time to come, with its
consequent effects on financial intermediation and disintermediation.

11

DOES TIGHT MONEY

DISCRIMINATE

AGAINST HOUSING?

Countercyclical monetary policy has often been accused of having "discriminatory" effects on the housing market. It is argued that tight money has its greatest impact on residential construction. In boom periods, when money is tightened and interest rates rise, home-building gets strangled. Subsequently, in recessions, when money eases and interest rates fall, home-building zooms ahead at an unnaturally rapid pace.

As a result, employment in the construction industry is unstable; workers try to even out their incomes over time by restrictive entry requirements and work rules; and entrepreneurs are discouraged from mechanization and modernization. All of which, it is alleged, leads to lower productivity in the housing industry than elsewhere in the economy. We are in the last half of the twentieth century but still building homes as though we were in the first half of the nineteenth. Low-cost housing seems impossible to construct and rents across the board, on both new and existing dwellings, are higher than they need be.

Is home-building indeed that fickle? If so, why? Can anything be done about it? *Should* anything be done about it?

The Truth about Housing

On the basis of the evidence, the contention that home-building is a foul-weather friend is difficult to deny. When GNP is bursting at the seams, construction tends to slacken; during downturns in overall business activity, the housing industry tends to expand. Of all the components of GNP, the record indicates that residential construction has experienced the greatest cyclical variability during the postwar years.

The chart on the next page traces residential construction as a per cent of GNP from 1951 through 1966. The shaded areas represent periods of recession in general business conditions, from the peaking out of the boom at the start of the shaded area to the trough of the recession at the end.

Home-building typically starts up during, or in some cases shortly after, a recession. Each of the shaded recession areas shows home-building swinging up except for 1960–1961, and in that case it started to rise within a few months after the recession trough had been reached. The peaks in home construction then occurred in 1955, 1959, and 1963—in other words, shortly after the recession—easy money years of 1954, 1958, and 1961.

On the other hand, during those years of highest overall employment and bubbling prosperity, which are typically the years just *before* the shaded areas start—as 1952–1953, 1956–1957, 1960, and 1966—residential construction is usually taking a nosedive. These boom periods are the very

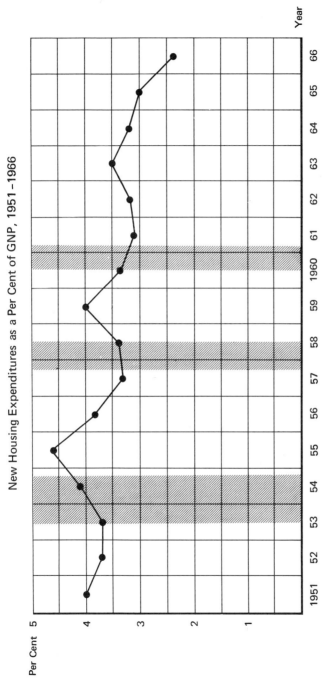

New Housing Expenditures as a Per Cent of GNP, 1951–1966

Shaded areas indicate periods of recession, from peak to trough, in general business conditions.

years when other kinds of spending, for example, consumer durables and business plant and equipment, are generally at or near their peak. But housing does not follow suit. As resources turn to making automobiles, television sets, and machine tools, the construction of homes takes a back seat. Indeed, the impact of the credit crunch of 1966 on home-building was so great that housing starts dropped to a twenty-year low despite a record number of family formations; sales of existing homes fell off; and many contractors and realtors went out of business.

Why? What causes these fluctuations in the housing market, fluctuations that appear to be so closely related to the actions of the central bank?

Interest-Rate Ceilings and the Supply of Housing Funds

During periods of tight money and rising interest rates, the supply of funds to the mortgage market is drastically curtailed. This sharp reduction in funds available for home-financing can be traced to two sources: the statutory interest-rate ceilings on mortgages, and the ceilings (such as Regulation Q) imposed on the rates that savings-type financial intermediaries are permitted to pay to attract deposits.

As the Federal Reserve begins to apply pressure on financial markets, interest rates start to go up on a wide variety of securities. Yields on government, municipal, and corporate bonds all begin to rise. Interest rates on mortgages go up with them. A housing contractor or potential home-buyer who wants to borrow mortgage money finds himself competing for the available supply of funds against many other potential borrowers—the federal government, state and local governments, corporations, even consumers. If competing rates go up, he must pay more as well or be outbid.

But if this general escalation of rates continues for any length of time, mortgage rates will sooner or later bump into the statutory ceilings imposed by the federal government on FHA and VA mortgages and by state governments under usury laws. And then the game is over and the marbles go elsewhere. For if other rates continue to climb but such ceilings prevent mortgage rates from doing so, lenders, naturally enough, begin to reduce their commitments to mortgage financing and instead place their funds in other higher-yielding securities, such as corporate bonds, where no rate ceilings exist.

Life insurance companies, for example, are likely to divert funds formerly earmarked for mortgages into corporate bonds. Similarly, commercial banks will switch out of mortgage lending and into business loans or municipal bonds. It is ironic that the FHA-VA ceilings and the usury laws, originally enacted to protect the small home-buyer and enable him to get cheap mortgage financing, have succeeded primarily in curtailing the availability of mortgages during periods of tight money.

Nor are these the only rate ceilings that are involved. Interest-rate ceilings on deposits at savings intermediaries compound the vulnerability of the mortgage market.

The two major mortgage-financing institutions are savings and loan associations and mutual savings banks. As we saw in Chapter 10, when interest rates rise during a period of tight money, these institutions can compete for funds as long as they can continue to move their deposit rates up in tandem with market rates. But once they have raised the rates they pay on deposits to the maximum permitted by federal or state law, they can go no further. If market rates continue to advance, but deposit rates at savings institutions cannot, then savers, potential depositors, will start to find it more attractive to invest their funds directly in the capital markets, rather than depositing them in savings and loans or savings banks. Financial disintermediation!

Since individual investors are not large mortgage lenders, funds which might well have gone into the mortgage market had they been deposited in a savings and loan association now move directly into stocks or bonds. The supply of funds available for mortgage lending dries up. This occurred most dramatically in 1966, when the savings and loan associations and savings banks lost funds not only to direct investment but also to the commercial banks.

Both types of interest-rate ceilings have essentially similar effects. Under conditions of tight money and rising interest rates, they divert funds away from financial institutions and assets that have "artificial" rate ceilings imposed on them to those that do not. Banking regulations that set ceilings on the rates financial institutions are allowed to pay depositors periodically choke off the normal inflow of funds to those institutions. Even if, by chance, they do receive an inflow of funds and are permitted any choice in what to do with them, the FHA-VA ceilings on mortgage rates make it doubly unlikely that the money will end up in the hands of a potential home-owner or home-builder. Under such circumstances, the funds are much more likely to finance corporate, municipal, or government spending.

All this is only half the story. Another side of the coin, the nature of the *demand* for mortgage money, also contributes to the instability of residential construction.

The Sensitivity of Demand

In Chapter 6 we noted that residential construction spending appears to be much more sensitive to changes in interest rates than any other category of expenditure. In the Federal Reserve's econometric model of the economy, a one percentage point increase in long-term interest rates reduces housing expenditures by $3 billion after one year, while business plant and equipment spending is reduced barely half a billion dollars.

Why is the demand for housing so much more sensitive to changes in interest rates than other kinds of spending? There are probably two major reasons. First, interest is a much greater proportion of total outlay in home-buying than it is in shorter-lived investments, such as inventory investment or the purchase of manufacturing equipment. The longer the investment period—that is, the longer the money will be tied up in the investment—the larger interest costs loom as an element in total costs. As we noted in Chapter 9, if you buy a $20,000 home and obtain a mortgage for the full amount at 7 per cent interest for thirty years, you will be paying $28,000 in interest alone. If the mortgage rate rises to 8 per cent, this will add an additional $5,000.

Second, the demand for housing is probably more sensitive than other kinds of spending to interest-rate changes because it is families that are undertaking the investment rather than business firms, and families can more easily postpone such expenditures for a year or two. Business firms also invest in long-lived projects—heavy machinery, physical plant, and so on—in which interest costs bulk as large as they do in housing. But corporations face competitive pressures from rival sellers and frequently have no choice in the matter; often they must either make improvements and additions quickly or else risk losing their share of the market.

Although it is difficult to pinpoint such things, the contraction in housing during 1952–1953 and 1956–1957 (see page 119) appears to have been due primarily to the interest sensitivity of demand. There was no sharp reduction in savings flows to intermediaries during those two tight-money periods, hence no major reduction in the availability of mortgage funds attributable to that source, although the FHA-VA ceilings did play a not unimportant role. The same seems to be true of 1960.

In 1966, however, the downturn in construction was significantly reinforced by a virtual stoppage in the supply of mortgage money. The diversion of savings flows away from mortgage-minded institutions and into direct market purchases of securities—financial disintermediation—is evident from even a casual inspection of the data. In 1965, savings and loan associations received $8.5 billion in deposits; in 1966, they received only $3.6 billion. Mutual savings banks experienced a similar decline. In fact, just about all the net additions to deposits at these institutions during 1966 represented interest payments credited to already existing accounts, rather than an inflow of new money.

The reaction of home-buyers to changes in interest rates thus reinforces the reaction of potential suppliers of mortgage money. When rates fall or rise, the former revise their spending plans and the latter rethink their allocation of funds. Result: feast or famine in the building industry.

Can Anything Be Done about It?

Many suggestions have been made for ameliorating the differential impact of monetary policy on the mortgage market. Proposals to eliminate the instability in the *supply* of mortgage funds naturally revolve around such measures as elimination of the FHA-VA rate ceilings and removal of the ceilings on the rates financial institutions are permitted to pay depositors. Alternatively, one might only impose deposit ceilings on commercial banks and leave savings and loan associations and mutual savings banks, which put most of their money into mortgages, free to pay whatever they wish to attract funds. This would give the mortgage-oriented institutions a competitive advantage over the commercial banks, which typically hold only a fraction of their assets in the form of home mortgages. Other proposals are usually variations on the same theme, such as allowing savings and loan associations to compete in the capital market for funds by issuing negotiable bonds which would not be subject to deposit-rate ceilings.

Of course, since all of these suggestions concentrate on the supply side, the instability in housing will still remain if, in fact, the major destabilizing element is the interest-sensitivity of *demand*. The only way to do anything about that would be to eliminate the fluctuations in interest rates!

We could do this, or come close to it, if we stopped using monetary policy as an instrument of economic stabilization and concentrated on fiscal policy, a strategy some Keynesians appear to favor for a wide variety of reasons. To prevent inflation, we would then impose tight fiscal policy (a budget surplus, with high tax rates and cutbacks in government spending), instead of tight money. If that were done, interest rates could possibly remain low across the board, and the rate ceilings, being irrelevant, would not interfere with the flow of mortgage funds.

In a sense, home-building would be favored by a tight fiscal policy in much the same way that it is hurt by a tight monetary policy. (Consumer spending and government services would probably be penalized most by a tight fiscal policy, leaving home construction relatively unaffected.) We will return to the subject of monetary versus fiscal policy in Chapter 15.

Should Anything Be Done about It?

Assuming that we are able to stabilize residential construction over the cycle, which is not too probable, the question still remains: *Should* we try to do so?

It is not such a bad thing, once you think about it, for the economy to have a foul-weather friend. The fact that housing has slackened during boom periods has taken some of the extreme inflationary pressure off the boom. Equally important, the prompt revival of housing during recessions has made our postwar recessions much less severe than they might otherwise have been. From the point of view of the housing industry, its instability has caused serious problems; but from the point of view of the overall economy, it has been, at least to some extent, a blessing.

Furthermore, as we have pointed out, one of the reasons the housing industry is plagued by stop-and-go is the sensitivity of demand to interest rates. When rates rise, many potential home-buyers decide to postpone their purchases. Corporations and others, in effect, outbid home-buyers for the available funds. Under such conditions, resources, both financial and real, move to where they are most in demand, which is precisely the way a price system is supposed to operate. Interest rates are a price, after all, the price of borrowing money. Excessive interference with the free flow of funds and resources in response to changes in relative prices is likely to result in the misallocation of both.

In any event, if we are to stop inflation during boom periods, *some* spending has to give way. If it is housing that gives way more than other kinds of spending, that may be because the demand for it, as expressed through the price system, is less urgent than the demand for other goods and services. Monetary policy's *differential* impact against housing is not necessarily a *discriminatory* impact. The former implies that the choice is freely made by the community, while the latter implies that something unfair and sinister is afoot.

Perhaps the best way to find out which it really is would be to do away with all rate ceilings and other "artificial" impediments to the free flow of funds, and then sit back and watch what happens.

12

DOES MONETARY

POLICY AFFECT THE

STOCK MARKET?

Any civic or social club program chairman knows that if he announces that next week's meeting will feature a renowned speaker on "The Crisis in America's Cities," hardly anyone will show up. But if he announces that the topic will be "The Outlook for the Stock Market" and mentions a speaker no one ever heard of, the hall will be packed. It would be hard to find a subject that intrigues people more than the stock market. Everyone knows about stocks: how they always go up, and how they can make you rich. Thirty years ago everyone knew about stocks: how they always go down, and how they can make you destitute.

Why do stock prices go up and down? Not so much particular stocks, like IBM or Xerox, but why does the entire stock market soar or shudder, with all stocks more or less rising or falling together?

It is a fact of life that the total supply of stocks in existence is more or less fixed. What changes is not so much the number of shares lying around—in vaults, under mattresses, and concealed between the pages of the family Bible—but the price of each.

For example, the market value of all the shares of stock now in existence amounts to something like $900 billion. Ten years ago it was about $450 billion, and ten years before that about $150 billion. And yet in the past twenty years corporations have raised relatively little money by issuing new stock, perhaps $30 or $40 billion at most. This means, and the word has obviously gotten around, that almost all of that $900 billion—maybe as much as $850 billion of it—represents price appreciation of existing shares.

The fact that the total supply outstanding is relatively fixed does not, of course, imply that the amount offered on the market need be fixed. People who have bought, and even some who haven't, can always sell. Thus in recent years stocks have been drifting from the hands of individual investors, who have been selling on balance, into the plush suites of institutional investors, who have been buying. A decade ago pension funds, mutual funds, and insurance companies held about 10 per cent of the market value of outstanding shares; now they hold over 20 per cent. But almost 80 per cent or over $700 billion is still held by individuals, about 25 million of them, and each and every one is out to make a killing.

Strangely enough, given the widespread interest in the stock market, economists have generally had very little to say about it. The most popular postwar college textbook, Paul Samuelson's *Economics,* is estimated to have sold over 2 million copies since it first appeared in 1948. Considering the royalties accruing to so popular an author, and a leading economist in the bargain, one would think he might have accumulated both the wherewithal and the trained experience to at long last unlock the secret of what makes the market tic.

But if Paul has found out, he isn't telling! The latest edition of *Economics* contains only three pages on the stock market (out of 794), which isn't much more than is devoted to social classes in the Soviet Union.

Some economists are less reticent than Professor Samuelson about letting us in on why stock prices fluctuate. Their explanations have ranged from the influence of sunspots on men's emotional behavior to the conspiratorial machinations of shadowy figures in high places. However, the explanations that are of most interest to us here deal with money and monetary policy.

Is it true, as some claim, that the elusive clue to movements in overall stock prices is to be found in changes in the money supply? Or does the secret lie, as others believe, in changes in monetary policy in general? If the former are correct, and to some extent the latter, perhaps all the paraphernalia that market analysts now so laboriously wrestle with for signs of the future can be put aside; the best tout sheet might turn out to be the weekly Federal Reserve statement.

A Money Supply View of Stock Prices

The belief that fluctuations in the money supply provide the key to movements in stock prices is based on the proposition that the money supply exercises a unique influence over virtually all economic activity, and that this influence can be pinpointed in terms of specific cause and effect.

Its application to the stock market is straightforward: Increases in the money supply give the public additional liquidity, part of which spills over into the stock market. Since the supply of existing stocks is more or less fixed, this incremental demand raises their price. Some stocks will go up more than others, and some will go down, depending on the prospects for particular companies, but overall the average of stock prices will rise.

Conversely, decreases in the money supply—or increases at a rate slower than necessary to accommodate the cash needed to finance the transactions of an expanding economy—leave the public with shortages of funds. Result: among other things, a cutback in stock purchases. This reduced demand for stocks lowers their price, and a concurrent increased desire to sell them (to get cash, which is in presumed short supply) adds further downward pressure.

Conclusion: higher money supply, higher stock prices; lower money supply, lower stock prices. The elapsed time between the change in the money supply and the reaction in the stock market is said to average about two months in the case of an upturn, slightly over a year in the case of a downturn. Like many single-cause explanations in economics, this view of stock prices contains too much truth to ignore, but not enough to make it very reliable in the clutch.

Consider 1929, and the couple of years before and after. From mid-1927 to mid-1928, the money supply increased by 1.6 per cent; from mid-1928 to mid-1929, it increased by 1.2 per cent. The stock market, meanwhile, going its merry way, *doubled*.

In the next two years, from mid-1929 to mid-1931, the money supply contracted by about 5 per cent each year. If the stock market was merely reacting to changes in the money supply, it was by all odds the biggest overreaction in history, because the proverbial bottom dropped out and the market promptly lost all the gains it had made in the previous two years and then some. Compared with *that* kind of overreaction, Mayor Daley's minions appear more wishy-washy than Charlie Brown.

Furthermore, it is not at all clear precisely what is cause and what is effect. Did the market crash because, among other things, the money supply contracted? Or did the money supply contract because the market crashed (as banks called speculative margin loans and demand deposits were wiped off the books)? The latter explanation is as logical as the former.

The 1929 market collapse, as many see it, was due to a number of interrelated factors: an unwarranted mood of euphoric optimism prior to the crash, excessive speculative activity, fundamental weakness in underlying business conditions, and so on. The money supply, if it influenced the break at all, did so only as one among many causes.

None of which is meant to imply that the money supply was or is unimportant. If it had been rapidly and forcefully restored to its 1929 level by 1930, or even 1931, the depression that was initiated by the stock market collapse would probably not have been either as severe or as long as it turned out to be. That the Federal Reserve stood by, wringing its hands, while the money supply declined by *30 per cent* from 1929 to 1933, undoubtedly intensified and prolonged what we now call the Great Depression. But that is a very different thing from saying that movements in the money supply caused or could have given one even a vague idea of the heights or the depths to which stock prices went in the years 1927 to 1931. As a matter of fact, most of the drop in the money supply occurred *after* 1931; by that time, however, the market was too weary to do any reacting, either over or under.

To come closer to the present, in 1940 the stock market

fell 15 per cent even though the money supply was then rising 15 per cent (on top of a similar rise the year before). In 1962, again, the market tumbled despite an increasing money supply.

On other not infrequent occasions, declines in stock prices *were* preceded or accompanied by declines in the money supply, as in 1957 and 1960. And often increases in stock prices were indeed associated with increases in the money supply, as in 1967 and 1968.

In at least some of these instances, however, both stock prices and the money supply might conceivably have been reacting to a third causal force, perhaps an upturn in business conditions stimulated by the outbreak of war ( ) peace ( )—check one—a spurt in consumer spending, or something else. An improvement in business conditions, regardless of cause, typically leads to an expansion in bank business loans, and thereby to a larger money supply; and to brighter profit prospects, and thereby higher stock prices. As the history of business cycles indicates, such upswings (or downturns) are capable of generating a cumulative push that can work up considerable momentum, carrying *both* the money supply and stock prices along with it.

The chart on page 135 provides some idea of the pitfalls involved in reading a cause-and-effect relationship into two sets of statistics simply because they move together. The heavy line indicates the movement of stock prices, annually, from the end of 1960 through the end of 1966, using stock prices at the end of 1960 as the base (= 100).

The thin dashed line, on a similar index basis, is the movement of the money supply annually, also from the end of 1960 through the end of 1966. Over this particular six-year period, changes in the money supply clearly bore little relationship to turning points in stock prices.

Finally, the chart also includes a third line (W). Its movements are obviously closely related to changes in stock prices. Almost without exception, the line labeled W and the line tracing stock prices move up and down together.

Cause and effect? The line labeled W, make of it what you will, is an annual index (1960 = 100) of the number of times members of the Washington Senators baseball team struck out, each year, over the period 1960 through 1966. (Source: The Sporting News's *Official Baseball Guide and Record Book,* Annual, 1960–1966.) For at least these years, evidently, an investor trying to forecast turning points in the stock market would have been better off spending his time reading the box scores instead of the money supply figures.

However, upon reflection, perhaps this is no accidental relationship, after all. Might it be statistical confirmation of the popular suspicion, heretofore unproven, that the affluent modern ballplayer pays more attention to his investments than to his batting average?

Monetary Policy and Wall Street

Once we expand our horizon to encompass more than the money supply alone, there seems to be general agreement that monetary policy, broadly viewed, does at times have a considerable influence on the stock market. The consensus appears to be that it is by no means the only influence, and often is far overshadowed by other forces and events; nevertheless, it is widely believed that on balance monetary policy has had a substantial effect on stock prices at times in the past, especially the recent past, and is likely to continue to do so in the foreseeable future.

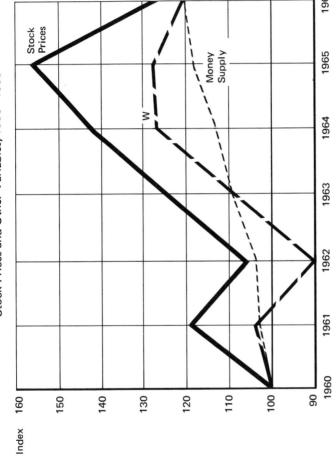

Stock Prices and Other Variables, 1960 –1966

Stock Prices = Dow-Jones Industrials, monthly closing averages for December of each year (December 1960 = 100).
Money Supply = Demand deposits plus currency, monthly averages for December of each year (December 1960 = 100).

This is quite aside from the power the Federal Reserve has to set margin requirements on stock purchases. In an attempt to prevent a repetition of the speculative wave, financed heavily with borrowed funds, that had carried the market to dizzy heights in 1928 and until the Fall of 1929, Congress, in the 1930's, authorized the Federal Reserve to impose margin (or minimum downpayment) requirements on the purchase of stocks. If the margin requirement is 100 per cent, no borrowing at all is permitted. If it is 80 per cent, that much of one's own cash must be put up when buying a security, and only the remaining 20 per cent can be financed by borrowing from a bank or a broker. Of course, you could finance the entire amount by borrowing from your brother-in-law and no one would be the wiser (except perhaps, in the long run, your brother-in-law).

High margin requirements probably have helped restrain speculation in stocks, particularly by those who could least afford it. Nevertheless, if the Federal Reserve had only this device to influence the market, it would be relying on a weak reed indeed. Margin requirements are 100 per cent at Santa Anita and Hialeah, but, at last report, speculative activity by those who could not afford it as well as by those who could appeared to be unimpaired.

Surprisingly, perhaps, it is in the recent past, rather than ten, twenty, or thirty years ago, that the impact of overall monetary policy on stock prices is most clearly visible. The credit squeezes of 1966 and 1969 are prime examples. During 1966, for instance, the money supply increased gradually, although irregularly, so that a strict Monetarist might question whether monetary policy was really very tight. But bankers, businessmen, and the general public had no such doubts; nor did the financial writers, who labeled the episode "The Great Credit Crunch of 1966." Credit availability was sharply curtailed, interest rates on fixed-income securities soared, and stock prices tumbled. The stock market fell 15 per cent during the year, despite continued inflation and booming business conditions—a rather clear indication of the potency of tight money when applied vigorously (indeed, too vigorously, many said).

The easy money policy that prevailed during 1967 and most of 1968 was accompanied by a rapid and lengthy upturn in the stock market. Nevertheless, one cannot be sure, under such circumstances, whether the extent of the rise in stock prices should be attributed to easy money or to the highly prosperous state of the economy. The subsequent reimposition of tight money late in 1968, however, and the prompt and substantial drop in the market that followed in 1969, even in the face of a step-up in the pace of inflation, made it plain that today the Federal Reserve has a significant impact on the stock market, especially during periods of tight money.

During the three decades from the early 1930's to the early 1960's, the reaction of the stock market to monetary policy was less prompt and less predictable than it has recently become. During those years, stocks frequently seemed to go their own way, regardless of what the central bank was doing. Not so any more.

There are two reasons for this change. First, the central bank has recently been acting with more authority than it did previously. In retrospect, during the 1950's and early 1960's, when the Federal Reserve was just getting its feet wet once again after almost twenty years of virtual inactivity, a wiggle in long-term bond rates would cause it to beat a hasty retreat. It was afraid to probe too far for fear of starting a recession. An increase in interest rates on long-term government bonds from 3½ to 4 per cent was considered a hazardous venture.

The credit squeeze of 1966, however, gave the monetary authorities a different perspective. Prices fell on long-term government bonds to the point where effective interest rates approached 5 per cent—not so high by today's standards, but the equivalent of Mount Everest then—and yields on some intermediate-term treasury bonds went over 6 per cent. The economy thrashed and strained, but it did not collapse. It proved to be more resilient than many had supposed.

However, something else did happen. For the first time in a generation, many investors became aware that such things as bonds existed. And that, under certain conditions, they were more attractive additions to one's portfolio than stocks. The rise in bond interest rates (which means a fall in bond prices) thus had repercussions in the stock market; some individual and institutional investors held off buying stocks, or sold some they had, and bought bonds instead, thereby driving stock prices down as well.

In theory, bond and stock prices *should* move together in precisely that way. As substitutes for each other, if the price of B falls some buyers should switch out of A and into B, thus lowering the price of A also. For similar reasons, if the price of B rises, the price of A should rise too.

However, during the 1950's, this relationship did not hold very closely. For most of that decade, interest rates on bonds were slowly rising, cautiously adjusting upward from artificially low war and postwar levels. Slowly rising bond interest rates imply slowly falling bond prices. Stock prices, on the other hand, were ebullient during most of the decade.

With yields on bonds and stocks now at more realistic levels relative to each other, the sympathetic relationship between the two has reasserted itself and is apt to continue into the future. From now on, when the Federal Reserve bangs bonds around, stocks are likely to get a nosebleed.

The second reason why monetary policy affects stock prices more today than ten or twenty years ago is simply that the Federal Reserve has made believers out of many former skeptics. If the Federal Reserve is ineffectual, who cares? But if monetary policy is effective in influencing the course of the economy, then a lot of people care a great deal. Today, many more financial analysts and observers of economic trends are persuaded that the central bank is able to achieve its announced objectives, or at least come reasonably close, than thought so a decade or two back.

Since stock prices presumably reflect views of future business conditions, if the Federal Reserve is believed to have an impact on the economy then what the Federal Reserve does will have an impact on the stock market. What really matters, of course, when it comes to the stock market, is not so much whether monetary policy actually is effective, but whether people think it is. Only a few think the monetary authorities are all-powerful, but many are convinced they are potent enough to worry about.

13

MONEY IN

INTERNATIONAL

FINANCE

The United States has had a deficit in its international balance of payments almost every year since 1949, which, as everyone knows, is a Bad Thing. As a result, we have been losing gold steadily, and *this,* it goes without saying, is an even more Serious Matter. We were the proud owners of 700 million ounces of gold in 1949, and now we have only about 300 million ounces left.

What to do?

An international "balance of payments" is an accounting record of all payments made across national borders. For each country, it shows the payments made to foreigners and the receipt of funds from them, in the same way that a family might keep a record of all its expenditures and receipts. Americans make payments to others, for example, when we import foreign goods, buy foreign securities, lend to other countries, build factories on the outskirts of London or in the suburbs of Rome, or travel abroad on our summer vacations. On the other side of the ledger, we take in money when foreigners pay us for our exports, buy our stocks or bonds, or visit the Grand Canyon.

A deficit in our balance of payments is no different from a deficit in a household's budget. It means that we have been paying out more money abroad than we have been taking in, possibly because we have been importing more than we have been exporting, or because more Americans are visiting Paris or London than foreign tourists are taking in the sights of Keokuk or Kalamazoo. Foreigners thereby accumulate more dollars than they need for their payments to us, and in the ordinary course of events some of their extra dollars are presented to the United States Treasury with a polite but firm request that they be exchanged for gold. You and I cannot get gold for our dollars, but the Treasury stands ready to promptly if not happily honor all official foreign requests at the rate of one ounce of gold for every $35 tendered.

Contrary to popular impression, the price of gold is not ordained by God. The price of $35 an ounce is an arbitrary price, set on January 31, 1934 by Franklin Delano Roosevelt (who, regardless of what you may have heard, was not the Deity). Before that, it had been $20.67 an ounce, set just as arbitrarily on March 14, 1900, by William McKinley (who certainly was not).

With 700 million ounces in Fort Knox, valued at $35 an ounce, we owned about $25 billion worth of gold in 1949. The 300 million ounces we still have left, at $35 an ounce, is worth less than half that—only about $10 billion. An obvious way to recoup our losses is to raise once again the price of gold, just as we did in 1934, this time to say $85 an ounce. We would then—presto!—have almost $25 billion worth of gold, as much as we had twenty years ago. In fact, if every country followed our imaginative leadership and raised the price of gold along with us, then *everyone* could have more gold. This would make the whole world richer overnight and automatically solve what is known as the international liquidity problem, a subject on which we will have more sage observations in Chapter 14.

In financial circles, unfortunately, this is known as Bad Thinking. It is called Devaluation, and for a country even to contemplate this possibility is universally recognized as a Humiliating Experience. Although there may be some misguided souls who might be willing to suffer a degree of humiliation for the sake of a $15 billion windfall, a succession of presidents, secretaries of the Treasury, Federal Reserve chairmen, and other Recognized Authorities have assured the rest of us that under no circumstances would they subject the American people to such an indignity.

In any event, while Devaluation might temporarily restore the value of our gold hoard, it would not necessarily affect our chronic balance-of-payments deficit—the fact that every year we pay out more than we take in. One remedy to cure that situation, a remedy invariably proposed by many in the international financial community and occasionally echoed by some here at home, is the old-fashioned hickory stick treatment.

The Discipline of the Balance of Payments

Balance-of-payments disciplinarians believe that to spare the rod is to spoil the child. Their recommendations as to how we should go about restoring equilibrium in our international accounts are appropriately strict: The Federal Reserve should administer the hickory stick by contracting the money supply and raising interest rates until tight money succeeds in reducing GNP and lowering wages and prices. It is difficult to estimate how much unemployment this might involve—perhaps 10 per cent of the labor force, at a minimum.

With a depression-level GNP, the incomes of Americans would be so low that we would be hard put to afford such "luxuries" as travel abroad and the purchase of so many foreign products. In addition, there would be relative price effects: With lower costs and prices in the United States, the relatively more expensive foreign goods will discourage Americans from buying so many Volkswagens and Japanese transistor radios, thus reducing our imports. The lower price-tags here would similarly encourage foreigners to buy more of our now cheaper goods and services, thereby expanding our exports. Less imports and more exports: We will be paying out less money abroad and taking in more, thus eliminating our balance-of-payments deficit and putting an end to our gold outflow.

At the same time, it is expected that purely financial flows would reinforce these effects. The higher interest rates the Federal Reserve induces here would bring in some foreign money seeking our attractive-yielding securities, and domestic money that had formerly been invested in foreign securities would presumably now stay home and buy American stocks and bonds.

This is called Defending the Dollar. Obviously, it is not a pleasant process, involving as it does tight money to induce heavy unemployment—heavy enough to wring lower wages and prices out of the economy—and a shrinking GNP. It is clear that it is based on the well-known Rocky Marciano Principle, that the best defense is a good offense: We defend the dollar by attacking the economy.

Professor Marciano thus takes his place in the Annals of

Economics, right behind Professor Phillips, of Phillips Curve fame (see Chapter 4); Professors Gurley and Shaw, of Gurley-Shaw Thesis renown (see Chapter 10); and Professor E. J. Finagle, discoverer of Finagle's Law ("inanimate objects are out to get us"). Of course, like all firm discipline, the Marciano Principle is administered reluctantly and only for our own good. Rest assured, it would hurt the Federal Reserve more than it would hurt the economy; the Federal Reserve said so itself when, on the basis of this sort of reasoning, it *raised* the discount rate from 1½ per cent to 2½ per cent on October 9, and then to 3½ per cent on October 16, of the year 1931. (It might be noted that by 1931 the Great Depression was something more than a speck on a far-distant horizon; GNP had already fallen far below its 1929 level.)

Fluctuating Exchange Rates

Another possible cure for a balance-of-payments deficit, one that does not clash so violently with the goals of high employment, stable prices, and economic growth, is to permit greater flexibility in the price of foreign money (or, what amounts to the same thing, in the foreign price of dollars). Currently, one British pound costs Americans $2.40, one Italian lira costs us sixteen cents, one Mexican peso costs eight cents, and so on. Under the present world monetary system, such exchange rates are fixed by international agreement under the overall supervision of the International Monetary Fund, although this supervision is not strict enough to prevent unilateral exchange-rate alterations when nations decide it is in their interest to do so.

Instead of the present system, exchange rates could be unpegged and left free to fluctuate from day to day in accordance with supply and demand conditions for each particular country's money. An increase in the *supply* of British pounds would lower their price, say from $2.40 to $2.00 a pound; an increase in the *demand* for Mexican pesos would raise their price, say from eight cents to sixteen cents a peso. This is not permitted under existing international monetary arrangements.

A deficit in our balance of payments, remember, means that we are paying out more money abroad than we are taking in. American importers are paying out more dollars for tiny cars and huge radio-phonograph consoles than foreigners need to buy the wheat and ball-point pens that we are exporting to them. Result: An excess supply of dollars is floating around in the world.

But if exchange rates were free to fluctuate in response to supply and demand, this excess supply of dollars, due to our sending so much money abroad, would depress the price of dollars to foreigners. Instead of the British having to pay one pound to get $2.40, something less than a pound would get them two of our dollar bills and four dimes; instead of the Mexicans having to pay one peso to get eight American pennies, perhaps half a peso would be enough to get them eight cents. Since foreigners could then get the same amount of our money for less of their own, our goods and services would become less expensive for them even though our domestic price-tags remained unchanged. It makes no difference to them whether our goods are less expensive for them because our price-tags are lower (the Marciano method) or because each United States dollar costs them less of their own money while our price-tags stay the same (the flexible exchange-rate method). In either case, our goods are cheaper for foreigners to buy and our exports are likely to expand.

From the American point of view, this *depreciation* of our money relative to other monies would mean that a British pound would now cost us something like $3.00 instead of $2.40, an Italian lira would cost perhaps twenty-five cents instead of sixteen cents, a Mexican peso possibly fifteen cents instead of eight cents. Since we now would have to pay more to get a British pound, an Italian lira, or a Mexican peso, foreign goods would become more expensive for us to buy. With foreign products costing us more, because foreign money costs more, our purchases from abroad—that is, our imports—would be likely to fall off.

Thus the end results are the same as though we had gone the Marciano route: less imports and more exports. We would be paying out less dollars abroad because of our lower imports, and taking in more pounds and pesos as we receive payment for our enlarged exports, thereby putting an end to both the depreciation of the dollar in foreign exhange and the deficit in our balance of payments. However, we would be achieving these results by letting exchange rates decline while keeping our economy stable, instead of by sending the economy into a nosedive while keeping exchange rates stable.

Freely fluctuating exchange rates would be a sharp departure from existing international monetary arrangements, which pivot on the fulcrum of fixed exchange rates. By and large, most academic economists, both Monetarist and Keynesian, lean toward exchange rate flexibility. Most bankers and government officials, on the other hand, seem to favor the present system. The proponents of fixed rates argue that rate flexibility would create so much risk and uncertainty that it would seriously inhibit international trade. Advocates of rate flexibility reply that fixed rates often create so much disruption at home that they seriously inhibit *domestic* trade —that is, the production of goods and services (GNP).

A possible middle ground that has won some adherents is to permit exchange rates to fluctuate within a predetermined range, say 10 or 15 per cent above and below present fixed rates. In addition, those fixed rates themselves might be altered in some agreed-upon gradual and orderly manner over a long time span.

Complications for Domestic Monetary Policy

The persistence of our balance-of-payments deficit has not made life any easier for the Federal Reserve. The central bank has ignored suggestions—usually from abroad—that it apply the Marciano Principle and set things right forthwith. The raising of the discount rate in 1931 has not been forgotten. But neither can the Federal Reserve bring itself to completely disregard the balance of payments when formulating domestic monetary policy, especially during periods of easy money.

In 1961, for example, the Federal Reserve moderated its easy money stance and allowed short-term interest rates to rise. Its intent was to let short rates rise to forestall an outflow of funds abroad—seeking more attractive yields on foreign securities—while at the same time keeping long-term interest rates stable at fairly low current levels to stimulate domestic business expansion.

While this attempt to twist the structure of interest rates was accomplished fairly successfully, it should be recognized that such a policy did to some extent limit the lengths to which the Federal Reserve was able to pursue its domestic easy money objectives. The Federal Reserve succeeded in keeping long-term interest rates steady while short-term rates rose, but it did not even *try* to lower long rates below prevailing levels. Under most circumstances, it simply is not possible to lower long-term interest rates appreciably without dragging short-term rates down with them. The desire to raise short-term rates because of balance-of-payments considerations thus restrained the vigor of easy money in the early 1960's.

During the tight money years of 1966 and 1969, the Federal Reserve again found itself affected by international flows of funds, although in a somewhat different way. In both of these years, the central bank's tight money policies were partially offset by large banks siphoning in so-called Euro-dollars from abroad through their foreign branches.

Euro-dollars are deposits of United States dollars in banks located abroad. Such deposits arose in the first place largely as the result of past American balance-of-payments deficits; foreigners acquired deposits in American banks as we paid them for our imports (their exports), and they in turn transferred the deposits to European banks. Such deposits then flowed back to this country in volume in both 1966 and 1969, when the Federal Reserve was putting substantial pressure on bank reserve positions. Large banks, primarily in New York City, borrowed the money back through their foreign branches to replenish the reserves the central bank was just as diligently trying to remove. In mid-1969, the slippage became so great that the Federal Reserve imposed reserve requirements on deposits arising from such transactions.

Is There a Solution?

Few in High Places—in this country, at least—recommend the thoroughgoing application of the Marciano Principle as the appropriate remedy for our balance-of-payments ills, and even fewer support the adoption of floating exchange rates. Instead, other devices have commended themselves to both Democratic and Republican administrations in the past decade, such as conjuring up different ways to measure the deficit (some of which occasionally make it almost invisible), levying a tax on American purchases of foreign securities, imposing "voluntary" restraints on loans and direct investments abroad by American banks and corporations, and placing ingenious obstacles in the way of Americans trying to make it through the International Departures gate at Kennedy International Airport (not to mention getting their baggage back into the country).

As is well known, our deficits have *not* been due to our inability to export as much merchandise as we import. We have been doing very well in that corner of the field, running heavy excesses of merchandise exports over imports and thereby taking in that much more money than we pay out. In general, we have not priced ourselves out of foreign markets, although we do seem to have priced ourselves out of some particular markets (steel, for example), and if our rate of inflation does not slow down, the problem is likely to spread. Thus far, however, American productivity has been able to keep most of our goods competitive on world markets despite our comparatively high wage levels.

Nevertheless, our net inflow of funds attributable to goods and services has been more than offset by the sum of net private capital outflows plus net government payments abroad. The private capital movements include direct investments in foreign countries by American corporations and the purchase of foreign securities by Americans. The government's payments abroad include loans, grants, and, most of all, military expenditures. These two categories—private capital movements and government payments—have so overwhelmed our net inflow of funds from goods and services that over the past decade the deficit in our overall balance of payments has run between $1 and $4 billion annually.

If any permanent improvement is to be made in our international payments position, it is clear that one of three things (or a combination of them) must take place: Our net export position on goods and services has to become even more "favorable" than it already is; our private capital movements abroad have to decline or be offset by a greater inflow of foreign capital into this country; or our government's commitments abroad, which are primarily military, must be reduced.

There is little chance that we will be able to achieve the first—an even larger excess of exports over imports—so long as we permit inflation to continue at the rate of 4 per cent or more a year. Already there is disturbing evidence that our merchandise net export position is deteriorating, rather than improving, under the double-barreled impact of advancing wages and prices in this country and accelerated productivity abroad.

Private capital movements give more hope for the future. Foreign investment in American securities appears to be increasing. The existing gap between our funds moving abroad via direct investment and loans, and foreign funds moving here, may very well narrow as the former stabilizes and the latter expands. In addition, the future income (interest and profits) that we can expect to earn on our foreign loans and investments gives promise of a swelling return flow of money back into this country.

The government's global military commitments, however, are the most—or the least—hopeful of all, depending on the direction we take in international affairs. As of early 1969, the United States government maintained 429 major and 2,972 minor overseas military bases in thirty foreign countries (*New York Times,* April 9, 1969). They were populated by a million of our servicemen stationed abroad, half a million of their dependents, and a quarter of a million foreign employees. If United States military bases are maintained on foreign soil for the protection of the countries in which they are located, one would think that the countries involved would pay us. However, for the most part it is we who pay them, thereby swelling the outflow of funds by about $3 billion a year.

If there are any lessons to be learned from the past decade, they are that we are overextended militarily . . . that powerful as we may be, we still cannot impose our will wherever and whenever we wish . . . that we cannot have both guns and butter simultaneously . . . and that our needs at home—racial tensions, poverty, urban blight, and environmental pollution—are too urgent to be put off any longer. If we have indeed learned these lessons, and act on them, then improvement in our balance of payments is likely to follow in due course.

14

WHAT ABOUT GOLD?

Once upon a time, long ago and far away, the natives of a small island in a remote part of the world had a monetary system of which they were justifiably proud. Although they lacked commercial banks and had no Federal Reserve, they had something that many people consider much more important—a monetary standard. It was not a gold standard. But it served the same purpose. It was a rock standard. Near the southeastern edge of the island, on a high cliff, sat a handsome and enormous rock, awesome to behold and thrilling to touch, and it was this that they decided should serve as "backing" for their money.

Naturally, the rock was too heavy, and indeed too valuable, to actually use as a means of payment. Instead, for circulating media itself, corresponding to our coins and dollar bills, they used special pieces of cloth. People had confidence in these because boldly inscribed on them were the words:

Will Pay to the Bearer on Demand One Dollar in Rock

The very fact that this statement was made meant that no one ever demanded any rock. The assurance that it was there was sufficient.

For many years all went well. The economy was simple

but prosperous, and those from the Great Civilizations across the sea who occasionally visited the island marveled at its stability and its thriving commerce. The natives were not reluctant to explain the reasons for their prosperity: hard work, thrift, clean living, and, above all, sound money. Sound as a rock.

Unfortunately, one night a severe storm struck the island. The inhabitants awoke the next morning to find the rock gone, evidently hurled into the sea by the furies of nature. Consternation! Panic! Luckily, however, they were saved from the potential consequences—worthless money and economic collapse—by an accident of fate that took place within the week. One of the younger natives, a child of no more than eight or nine, perched on the very cliff where the rock had once been, was looking at a rainbow arching far out over the horizon. Following it down, he suddenly saw—or thought he saw—the rock, fathoms deep, under the water.

After much excitement, it was finally ascertained that on very clear days, when the sea was calm and the sun at a certain angle, some who had especially strong eyes could see it. Those who could not, which included almost everyone, were assured by those who could that the outlines of the boulder were indeed discernible. And so, the backing still there, confidence in the money was restored, and, in a short while, the island became more prosperous than ever.

Of course, all the outstanding money had to be called in, so that the elders of the community could strike out the words:

Will Pay to the Bearer on Demand One Dollar in Rock

In their place was painstakingly inscribed:

Will Pay to the Bearer on Demand One Dollar
in Lawful Money

Now, if anyone brought in a piece of cloth to be redeemed, it would simply be exchanged for another piece of cloth. As it turned out, however, no one bothered. After all, with the backing assuredly there, the money obviously was as good as rock.

Gold at Home

Our own monetary system, of course, has always been much more rational. Until the early 1930's, all of our money was redeemable in gold at the United States Treasury. Every dollar bill, and for that matter every demand deposit as well, actually or implicitly bore the following inscription:

The United States of America
Will Pay to the Bearer on Demand One Dollar in Gold

Then, overnight, it was declared illegal for anyone in this country to have gold in his possession, except for industrial or dental purposes. Accordingly, the inscription on the currency was solemnly, officially, and duly altered to:

The United States of America
Will Pay to the Bearer on Demand One Dollar
in Lawful Money

In 1947, a literal-minded citizen of Cleveland, A. F. Davis, sent the Treasury a ten-dollar Federal Reserve Note and respectfully requested, in return, the promised ten dollars in "lawful money." He received back, by return mail, two five-dollar bills.

Seventeen years later, in 1964, the venerable inscription was finally removed from our currency. All that remains is an unpretentious observation: This note is legal tender for all

debts, public and private. Also (in considerably larger type):
In God We Trust.

Pursuing the same theme somewhat further: Until 1965
the Federal Reserve Banks were required to hold reserves in
the form of gold or warehouse receipts for gold (called gold
certificates). The amounts required were 25 per cent behind
member-bank deposits at the Federal Reserve Banks (member-bank reserves) and also 25 per cent behind all outstanding Federal Reserve Notes (most of our currency). These
gold or gold certificate reserves were considered the ultimate
backing behind our money, both demand deposits and
currency—the underlying foundation upon which our entire
monetary system was based.

Then, on March 3, 1965, the gold backing behind
member-bank reserves was quietly eliminated by Congress
and the president. Three years later, on March 19, 1968, the
corresponding gold reserve against currency was also abolished, just as casually. No one seems to care. The newspapers hardly mentioned it. Does this mean that we are
finally growing up?

All of which raises an intriguing question. There is, we are
told, about $10 billion worth of gold buried deep beneath
the surface of the earth in heavily guarded Fort Knox,
Kentucky. Have you ever seen it? Do you know anyone
who has? Do you *really* believe it is there?

Gold Abroad: International Liquidity

We seem to have broken free almost completely from our
superstitious attachment to gold here at home. We no longer
think we are being deprived of our constitutional rights be-

cause it is illegal to have gold in our possession, and we appear to be perfectly capable of transacting business without using little gold coins, the kind we had before 1933.

However, the same cannot be said of the world at large. Private citizens still hoard gold in many countries where there is no law against it, and in some countries where there is. And nations, including the United States, do the same, since they continue to settle up their net debts among themselves by playing house with small gold bars of a specified purity and weight. This is no doubt less harmful than many things nations do to each other, but it is still unfortunate, as well as irrational, if only because there simply is not enough gold on this planet for it to be a suitable medium of international exchange. Just as too little money within a country would inhibit domestic economic growth, so the scarcity of gold in the world poses a serious threat to the expansion of world trade, if mankind persists in using it as a means of international payments.

There is probably about $60 to $63 billion worth of gold in existence in the world today (roughly 1,700 million to 1,800 million ounces at $35 an ounce), not counting what is imbedded in molars or used in jewelry and by industry, for functional or ornamental purposes. The United States has $10 billion of it stashed away (we are told); other noncommunist governments and central banks have about $30 billion; and the remaining $20 to $23 billion, which is the part that has to be guessed at, is divided up in proportions no one knows between the official coffers of Communist Bloc nations (who do not reveal their gold holdings) and private hoards squirreled away by peasants and potentates scattered from France and Switzerland to India, Lebanon, and Kuwait.

The annual production of newly mined gold adds to this

total at the rate of only about $2 billion a year. Half of this comes from South Africa and the other half from all the rest of the world, including the Soviet Bloc. In many years, this is not sufficient to satisfy all the *nonmonetary* demands for gold, not to mention the monetary ones. Jewelers, dentists, and manufacturers use about half to three-quarters of a billion dollars worth a year, and hoarders frequently acquire and then promptly hide several billion dollars more. So even though newly mined output adds about $2 billion to the total supply every year, some years end with less gold on hand for worldwide *monetary* uses than was available when the year began.

Since nations insist on using it as a medium of international exchange, the scarcity of gold has meant a growing shortage of international liquidity. Just as individuals and business firms hold liquid cash to bridge the gaps between their receipt of funds and their expenditures, and to carry them over periods when inflows of funds are slack, so nations also need to hold an internationally acceptable means of payment for similar purposes. Such international liquid cash balances, usually called international reserves, are typically held in the form of gold because of its universal acceptability. With gold so scarce, however, many foreign countries have taken to holding a substantial proportion of their international reserves in the form of dollars. They acquire dollars when we run our deficits, and then they hold them as their cash balances instead of exchanging them for gold since dollars are just as acceptable as gold in settling international payments.

This means, however, that to a great extent the supply of international money depends on the vicissitudes of the American balance-of-payments position. When we have a deficit and pay out more money than we take in, international liquidity expands. But were we to correct our deficits and start running surpluses, taking in more money than we pay out, international liquidity would dry up—with potential restrictive effects on the volume of world trade.

The fact that many countries hold their international cash balances in the form of dollars instead of gold also explains why we hesitate to devalue—that is, raise the price of gold —even though if everyone did so it would ease the gold shortage overnight and automatically augment the supply of international liquidity. If the price of gold were doubled, to $70 an ounce, then there would be $120 to $126 billion worth of gold in the world instead of $60 to $63 billion, and every year $4 billion would emerge from the earth (preliminary to going back in again) instead of $2 billion. However, those nations that have been holding dollars instead of gold would be out in the cold. In a very real sense, given the irrationalities of the system, they have been helping us out by being content with dollars and not demanding gold. If we devalued, these countries would look more than a little foolish: If they ever did want gold, they would have to pay twice as much.

On the other hand, those countries that have always refused to hold dollars and insisted on gold instead would benefit greatly from devaluation. Their large gold stock, so wisely accumulated, would double in value. Other major beneficiaries would be the world's leading gold producers, South Africa and the Soviet Union.

Many alternatives have been proposed for enlarging international liquidity without relying on gold mining, United States balance-of-payments deficits, or a worldwide increase in the price of gold (worldwide devaluation). Several proposals would establish a supranational central bank, empowered to create international reserves via open-market operations in much the same way that the Federal Reserve creates money domestically.

Another plan, less drastic than the others, has recently been adopted. It permits the International Monetary Fund— an institution established in 1945 primarily for the purpose of maintaining exchange-rate stability—to create several billion dollars of a new form of international money known as "paper gold" or Special Drawing Rights (SDRs). These can be used to settle international payments in the same way as dollars or gold, and are a purely man-made bookkeeping form of addition to existing international reserves. Although a small step, it nevertheless represents the first sign, however hesitant, of an inching away from mysticism in international monetary affairs.

PART III

An Overview

15

MONETARY POLICY

VERSUS

FISCAL POLICY

The promoter of a match billed as Monetary Policy versus Fiscal Policy would surely be able to call this encounter the Main Event for the Heavyweight Title. Twenty years ago, however, such a contest would not have made even the preliminaries in the Featherweight division. A forfeit would have been declared in favor of fiscal policy. The reason? It would have been generally believed that monetary policy was unable to defend itself.

The dramatic resurgence of monetary policy since the late 1940's and early 1950's rivals the most classic of comebacks. Two decades ago, monetary policy was relegated to the subservient role of sweeper before the chariot of the Champion. Its functions were to keep bank reserves plentiful and the market for government securities firm, so that interest rates could remain low and nothing impede the right of way of the Great Man. Fiscal policy, alone, in all its Glory, would promote full employment, stabilize prices, ensure economic growth, and eliminate poverty. The reader who thinks that this might be an exaggeration, which it probably is, should reread some of the more exuberant literature typical of that era.

Today they march to a different tune. Although some die-hard fans of fiscal policy still boo each move of the monetary authorities, calling every punch a foul and every feint unfair, their enthusiasm is not what it once was, and their ranks have dwindled with the passage of time. Government economists now place monetary policy on an equal footing with fiscal policy in the pursuit of national economic objectives. Some academic economists even go so far as to argue that monetary policy should be *the* instrument of economic stabilization, that the impact of fiscal policy is uncertain, at best. As we indicated earlier, much of the controversy centers about the debate between the Monetarists and the Keynesians.

How Fiscal Policy Works

According to the Monetarists, a change in the money supply will alter aggregate spending and GNP by a predictable amount, since the velocity of money is quite stable. Thus they contend that monetary policy is a much more effective instrument than fiscal policy.

The Keynesians, on the other hand, are skeptical about the reliability of the relationship between the money supply and GNP. As they view it, a change in the money supply can alter aggregate spending only to the extent that it first changes interest rates or the availability of credit, and then only if business or household spending is sensitive to those changes. There is no direct link between the money supply and spending. Put briefly, the relationship between the money supply and GNP is seen as tenuous and variable since fluctuations in the velocity of money may counteract changes in its supply.

In Keynesian eyes, changes in government spending or taxation—the primary tools of fiscal policy—*do* have a direct and fairly predictable impact on GNP. An increase in government spending raises GNP immediately. It also induces additional "multiplier effects" via the consumption-GNP link. As GNP rises due to an initial injection of government expenditure, consumers receive more income; they spend a fraction of this increased income, which causes GNP to go up even further. For example, if government spending rises by $10 billion, income (or GNP) automatically goes up by $10 billion. Out of this larger income, consumers will then spend a predictable fraction, say four-fifths or $8 billion. Since spending by A is income to B, GNP goes up by this $8 billion as well. Out of this, consumers then spend another four-fifths or $6.4 billion. By now, GNP has gone up $24.4 billion. Eventually this process will come to a halt as the successive increments in income and spending become smaller and smaller; but the end result will be an increase in GNP by some multiple of the original increase in government spending.

Changes in tax rates are seen as having a similar multiple impact on GNP. If tax rates are lowered, consumers are left with more disposable income. They spend a predictable fraction of this, causing a rise in GNP, which in turn induces additional consumer expenditure. Conclusion: To bring about an expansion in spending and GNP, we should increase government spending and/or lower tax rates—that is, create a budget deficit. Anti-inflation policy would call for the opposite: Reduce government spending and/or raise tax rates—that is, create a budget surplus.

It is important to note the central role of the consumption-income relationship in the Keynesian "multiplier" analysis. If consumer spending does not respond to changes in income, tax-rate changes would not affect spending or economic activity, and the "multiplier effects" of changes in government expenditure would be minimal.

Changes in government spending and/or tax rates can be implemented in many different ways. Government spending can be changed via military expenditures, outlays for education, urban renewal, farm price supports, medical research, the space program, or for any other specific government program. Tax receipts can be altered by changing the corporate income tax, the personal income tax, the investment tax credit, or any specific excise or sales tax.

While the impact of a change in any one of these tax or expenditure categories can be made virtually identical with a change in any other one, insofar as the arithmetic effect on GNP is concerned, profound social implications flow from which particular tax or expenditure program is or is not altered. For example, if we are experiencing substantial unemployment and a low rate of economic growth, and fiscal policy is decided upon as the appropriate remedy, a choice arises between lowering taxes and raising government spending. If we lower tax rates, the expansion in GNP will be brought about by private spending. If we increase government spending, this will give us more government services as well as more private purchases. Which alternative we choose should depend on the volume of government (social) services we want.

Going still further: If we decide that we should increase government spending, should it take the form of more money devoted to the space program or an expansion in urban renewal? When we are faced with inflationary pressures, should we cut back military expenditures or anti-poverty programs? To a certain extent, these are the issues that the rioting in the streets and disorders on the campus have been all about. Unfortunately, economists, as economists, are no more competent to decide among such alternatives than they are able, as we saw in Chapter 4, to adjudicate whether we should have more employment and less price stability or more price stability and less employment. Once again, the choices involve moral issues and personal value judgments that are quite outside the scope of economics. All the economist, as an economist, can do—and it is not without some value—is explain why, if we are already reasonably close to full employment, we cannot increase *both* military expenditures *and* urban renewal programs and still avoid inflation.

Measuring Fiscal Policy

Until now, we have discussed expansionary and contractionary fiscal policy in terms of deficits and surpluses in the federal budget. A budget deficit is expansionary and a budget surplus is contractionary. However, just as many widely used indicators of monetary policy are less than adequate (see Chapter 7), so there are also serious limitations in using the *current* deficit or surplus as a guide to the performance of fiscal policy.

The measurement problem stems from the fact that tax receipts, and hence the size of the deficit or surplus, vary with GNP. Congress sets tax *rates,* not receipts; receipts then go up and down with GNP. Given the level of government spending, when GNP rises, tax receipts increase and surpluses are automatically created (or deficits reduced). When

GNP falls, tax receipts decline and deficits automatically result. Thus, it is impossible to draw any meaningful conclusions regarding the stance of fiscal policy by comparing a budget surplus in one year, at one level of GNP, with a deficit in another year, at a different level of GNP.

For example, the existence of a deficit during a recession suggests, at first glance, that fiscal policy is expansionary. It may be, however, that the tax structure is so steep that it drives income (and thereby tax receipts) down to recession levels. A deficit may thus actually be the byproduct of a *contractionary* fiscal policy. The tax cut of 1964 was enacted primarily on the basis of such thinking, the intention being to reduce the "fiscal drag" on the economy. It was argued that the overly restrictive tax structure—with taxes rising too rapidly as GNP went up—made it virtually impossible for GNP to make any sustained headway.

The budget concept that *is* useful as an indicator of the impact of fiscal policy is called the full employment budget. The main problem in comparing deficits or surpluses in year X with year Y is that there are different levels of GNP in the two years. As the chart indicates, the idea of the full employment budget eliminates this problem. The full employment budget is defined as what the federal budget surplus (or deficit) *would be,* with the expected level of government spending and the existing tax structure, *if the economy were operating at the full employment level of GNP throughout the year.* In this context, a 4 per cent unemployment rate is usually considered full employment. This calculated measure, the full employment budget, can be used to evaluate the effects and the performance of fiscal policy more meaningfully than the actual state of the budget, whatever it might be. Indeed, as an indicator of fiscal policy, the full employment budget is a much less ambiguous policy measure than

The Full Employment Budget

Tax Receipts
and
Government
Spending

Government Spending

Actual
Budget

Balanced
Budget

Full Employment
Budget

Tax Receipts

Surplus

Deficit

Tax Receipts

Actual GNP in
1962

Full
Employment
GNP in 1962

GNP

any we thus far have been able to produce for monetary policy.

As an illustration, in 1962, GNP was well below its full employment potential. As the diagram indicates, this low level of GNP produced a poor tax harvest and, consequently, a deficit in the actual budget. Nevertheless, fiscal policy was hardly expansionary. In fact, it was quite the opposite; if GNP had been at the full employment level, or close to it, tax revenues would have risen so greatly that the *full employment budget* would have had a substantial surplus. Conclusion: The fundamental stance of fiscal policy was restrictive, not expansionary, and one reason for the high level of unemployment in 1962 was this impact of fiscal policy—even though the actual budget showed a deficit.

Thus, in a rare example of fiscal bravery, a tax cut was passed by Congress in 1964 despite the existence of a current budget deficit. A reduction in tax rates shifts the tax receipts line (in the diagram) downward and diminishes the full employment surplus. An increase in government spending also shrinks the full employment surplus. A tax-rate increase or a drop in government spending, both of which are restrictive actions, enlarge it. It is clear that changes in the full employment budget reflect basic *discretionary* changes in fiscal policy, as contrasted with movements in the actual budget, which can be the passive result of fluctuations in GNP.

Under circumstances such as we had in 1962, if the multiplier effects due to the consumption-income relationship (see page 165) are powerful enough, a tax cut (or an increase in government spending) will eventually succeed in increasing GNP sufficiently to convert an actual deficit into a balanced budget or an actual surplus.

This, of course, violates the most sacred canons of "traditional" (or pre-Keynesian) finance. According to the maxims of "orthodox" finance, an actual deficit is a signal to immediately set about balancing the budget by *raising* tax rates and/or *decreasing* government spending—this promptly drives GNP lower, thereby creating an even *larger* deficit, which makes matters worse all around.

Financial Aspects of Fiscal Policy

The fiscal policy mechanism described above is not the whole story. This is recognized by both Keynesians and Monetarists. The total impact on GNP of an expansionary fiscal policy cannot be fully ascertained until the method of financing government deficits is specified. Similarly, the net effect of a reduction in government spending and/or increases in tax rates cannot be fully calculated until the disposition of the surplus is taken into account.

When GNP goes up as the result of deficit spending, the public's need for day-to-day transactions money rises along with it. If the supply of money does not increase simultaneously, the public will find itself short of cash, will presumably sell off some financial assets in order to try to get additional money, and will thereby drive up the rate of interest. This may have an inhibiting effect on private investment spending and on home-building, partly offsetting the expansionary effect of the government's spending.

But a budget deficit can be financed in either of two ways. For one, the government might simply print money to finance itself. Since this is often frowned upon in the best of circles, its twentieth-century equivalent is used instead: The government sells its bonds to the Federal Reserve, which pays for them by creating brand-new checking accounts for the government's use. If this is done, the increased supply of money will probably be sufficient to satisfy the enlarged need for money and interest rates will not rise. In this case, there will be little or no offset to the expansionary impact of the deficit spending, and GNP will be able to rise without interference from the monetary side.

Alternatively, the deficit might be financed by the sale of government bonds to the public. Buy government bonds and help Defend Democracy! If this is done, however, the pressure on financial markets is actually intensified, since the increase in the supply of new bonds on the market drives up the rate of interest even further. Decreased investment spending will offset an even larger portion of the increased government spending. The net effect, according to the Keynesians, is still expansionary, although less so than in the case of money-financed deficits.

In any event, regardless of details, the important point is that the execution of fiscal policy is inextricably mixed up with monetary implications. The two cannot be separated.

The Monetarists versus the Keynesians

The Keynesian position is that any fiscal action, no matter how it is financed, will have a significant impact on GNP. Keynesians do not deny that interest rates are likely to rise as GNP goes up, unless new money is forthcoming to meet cash needs for day-to-day transactions. Thus, they admit that a deficit financed by money creation is more expansionary than one financed by bond sales to the public, and that both are more expansionary than increased government spending financed by taxation. However, Keynesians do not believe that the decrease in private investment spending caused by higher interest rates will be great enough to fully offset the government's fiscal actions. They think that the net effect will be significant, and in the right direction, regardless of what financing methods are used.

One reason for this conclusion is that higher interest rates themselves are seen as having dual effects. They may reduce private investment spending, although many Keynesians are skeptical about this; but they may also lead people to economize on their cash balances, thereby supplying part of the need for new transactions money out of formerly idle cash holdings, and here the Keynesians are True Believers. Put somewhat differently, even if a deficit is not financed by new money, the velocity of existing money will accelerate (in response to higher interest rates) so that it will be able to support a higher level of spending and GNP.

The Monetarist view, on the other hand, is that unless a budget deficit is financed by new money creation it will not alter GNP. Since velocity is seen as more or less constant, a direct link exists between the money supply and GNP. In order for GNP to rise, the money supply must expand.

If a fiscal deficit is financed by printing money, it will indeed increase spending and GNP. But according to the Monetarists, it is not the deficit that is responsible, it is the additional money. Furthermore, a deficit is a very clumsy way to go about increasing the money supply. Why not simply have the Federal Reserve engage in open-market operations? That would accomplish the same purpose, a change in the money supply, without getting involved in budget deficits or surpluses.

As the Monetarists see it, a fiscal deficit financed in any other way—as by selling bonds to the public—will not affect aggregate GNP. True, the government will be spending more. But others will wind up spending less. Net result: no change in total spending or in GNP.

The rise in government spending will initially increase GNP. However, this will increase the demand for cash for transactions purposes and drive interest rates up, and bond sales to finance the government's expenditures will drive rates up still further. The public will be buying government bonds and financing the government, instead of buying corporate bonds and financing business firms. The rise in interest rates will reduce private investment spending by as much as government spending is increased, and that will be the end of the story. Government fiscal policy, unaccompanied by changes in the supply of money, merely changes the proportion of government relative to private spending.

Anti-inflationary fiscal policy encounters similar objections from the Monetarists. An increase in tax rates that generates a fiscal surplus reduces private income and consumer spending. If the government destroys or simply holds the money, the tax revenue it has collected over and above its expenditures, then the surplus is accompanied by a reduction of the money supply in private pockets. Both Keynesians and Monetarists would agree that this is anti-inflationary, although for different reasons—the Keynesians because of the direct fiscal impact on consumer spending, with the tax increase reducing people's take-home pay, and the Monetarists because of the contraction in the money supply.

But if the government uses the surplus to retire part of the national debt, the funds flow back into the economy. The government retires debt by buying back its bonds. Bond prices are driven up, interest rates fall, and private investment spending increases. Keynesians would argue that GNP will still decline, that the debt retirement is a minor ripple on a huge wave. Monetarists, however, would say that private investment spending will increase until it replaces the cutback in consumer spending, leaving no net effect whatsoever on GNP.

As we stressed in Chapter 5, the fight between fiscal and monetary policy can be decided only by resort to the empirical evidence. The Keynesians claim that the power of fiscal policy was demonstrated by the success of the 1964 tax cut in bringing the economy up to a high level of employment. The Monetarists contend that fiscal policy alone is useless and that it was the rapid expansion of the money supply during the months preceding the tax cut that did the job. They also point to the failure of the 1968 tax surcharge to stop inflation. The Keynesians respond by asserting that acceleration of the war in Vietnam undid the impact of the 1968 tax increase.

Frustrated, let us turn to the Federal Reserve's econometric model that we discussed in Chapter 6. Unfortunately, it is also ambiguous. An increase of $1 billion in government spending raises GNP by about $3.5 billion after one year, according to the model, while a $1 billion increase in bank reserves raises GNP by only $2 billion over the same time interval. After three years, however, their relative effectiveness is reversed; the impact of fiscal policy is no greater than after one year, while monetary policy gathers momentum and becomes considerably more powerful in the second and third years.

Perhaps the econometric model suggests the outline of a possible compromise, a draw. Both fiscal policy and monetary policy affect GNP. Fiscal policy seems to be more powerful in the short run; monetary policy appears to be more powerful in the long run. Of course, this satisfies the extremists in neither contingent.

Who gets the verdict has implications far beyond flattering the egos of economists in the two camps. If we are in a recession and use easy money to raise GNP, interest rates will fall and private investment and home-building will expand. On the other hand, if we use fiscal policy—lowering tax rates or increasing government spending—consumer spending or social services will be favored instead.

If we are in a boom and want to reduce aggregate spending, tight money will hit housing hard, tight fiscal policy probably will not. If a vibrant housing industry is important for national social and economic welfare—on the theory that the American Dream consists of each citizen owning his own home with a well in the backyard—perhaps we should rely mainly on easy money to stop recessions and mainly on tight fiscal policy to halt inflation.

A rational overall stabilization policy would evaluate all of these elements, and more, before embarking on a course of action. There are likely to be other side effects, some desirable, others undesirable. Often political considerations will be involved as well: It is difficult, for example, to raise taxes in an election year. Not to mention the influence that various pressure groups and vested interests are likely to bring to bear on such decisions.

In any case, the importance of *both* fiscal and monetary policy, and the numerous interrelations between them, makes it plain that there can be no clear-cut winner. If either fiscal policy or monetary policy is declared the victor, to the neglect and subjugation of the other, it is we who will be the losers.

16

SHOULD WE

WORRY ABOUT THE

NATIONAL DEBT?

"Personally," said President Eisenhower, in his State of the Union Message in 1960, "I do not feel that any amount can properly be called a surplus as long as the nation is in debt. I prefer to think of such an item as a reduction in our children's inherited mortgage."

In the same vein, Senator Harry F. Byrd, Sr., pondered the $275 billion national debt in 1955 and gloomily predicted: "The debt today is the debt incurred by this generation, but tomorrow it will be debt on our children and grandchildren, and it will be for them to pay, both principal and interest."

Debt worriers are fond of statistical computations. We now have a national debt of $360 billion (held in marketable and nonmarketable form by the public and by government agencies) and a population of 200 million. Conclusion: Every man, woman, and child in this country owes $1,800, whether he knows it or not. Every newborn infant starts life not only with a pat on the back but also with a debt of $1,800 hanging over his head.

Agonizing over the size of the public debt is one of our major national preoccupations. As the National Worry Meter (page 179) indicates, the most recent scientific poll of a stratified sample of our population showed that The National Debt ranks close to the top of all our worries. It is considered more worrisome than either Pornography or Communism, although it is still viewed as somewhat less of a problem than the two Worst Things we have to contend with, The Younger Generation and the breakdown in Law And Order.

Is the situation really all that bad? Are the debt worriers right when they warn us that, by passing on a national debt of $360 billion, we are burdening future generations with a weight it will be almost impossible for them to bear? Are they correct in cautioning us, with stern voices, that we are penalizing those as yet unborn by forcing them to pay for our own vices and follies?

The National Debt Equals the National Credit

The national debt is essentially the net result of past and present fiscal policy, mostly past. It is the sum of all past deficits, less surpluses, in the federal budget. A budget deficit requires that the government either print money or borrow to cover the deficit, and most modern governments choose to borrow (that is, sell government securities). As a result, we acquire a national debt, embodied in the form of government bonds; the total of government bonds outstanding *is* the national debt. It is increased by every additional deficit we incur and finance by issuing more bonds.

If it is a debt, we must owe it to someone. Indeed we

The National Worry Meter

Law and Order

The Younger Generation

The National Debt

90

80

70

Communism

60

Pornography

50

Worry Index

Automation

40

30

The Future of Baseball

20

The Military-Industrial Complex

10

Highway Fatalities

do—we owe it to ourselves. Almost all our government's bonds are internally held, that is, they are owned by citizens of the United States. Thus, while we the people (as the United States) *owe* $360 billion, we the people (as owners of government bonds) are simultaneously *owed* the same amount. A government bond is, after all, an asset for whoever buys it.

All evidences of debt must appear on *two* balance sheets, and government securities are no different from any other IOU in this respect. Every IOU appears on the balance sheet of the debtor, as a liability; but it also turns up, not surprisingly, on the balance sheet of whoever is holding it, its owner, this time as an *asset*. Thus, every liability necessarily implies the existence of a financial asset owned by someone else. For the same reason, every *financial* asset implies a corresponding liability on the part of someone else.

This accounting fact of life has interesting ramifications. It means, for one, that merely creating money cannot, in and of itself, make a country richer, a conclusion that always pleases conservatives. For after all, money is a financial asset, which implies that somewhere else there is a corresponding liability. If liabilities go up as rapidly as assets, the country as a whole (including both the government and the private sector) can be getting no richer.

Most of our money is in the form of demand deposits, which are liabilities of commercial banks. The part of our money that is in the form of coin or currency is a liability of either the United States Treasury or the Federal Reserve, depending on which agency issued it.

Thus merely creating money can hardly make a nation richer, no matter how much it creates. To become richer—to increase its net worth—a country must increase its output of *real* assets, its production of real goods and services. As conservatives like to point out, if we want to become wealthier, we must work harder and produce more. Printing money, per se, will not do it.

By the same token, however, exactly the same logic also implies that one of the conservatives' favorite incantations is equally false: namely, the belief that increasing the national debt makes a country poorer. Government bonds are liabilities to the government but are financial assets to whoever owns them. If the national debt increases, someone's financial assets go up as much as the government's liabilities. If assets rise along with liabilities, the country as a whole can be getting no poorer.

The very term *national debt* is thus a half-truth. If it is a domestically held debt, it could just as well be called the *national credit*. Both labels are half-truths. As with all liabilities, it is *both* a debt (to the borrower) *and* a credit (to the lender).

To become poorer—to reduce its net worth—a country must reduce its holdings of real assets, curtail its production of *real* goods and services. Increasing the national debt, no matter how high, cannot in and of itself make a country poorer.

Nor does an increasing national debt, just because of its size, impose a burden on future generations. As long as the debt is held internally, neither the interest nor the principal represents a dead weight on the backs of our children and grandchildren. The taxes that must be raised to pay the interest are merely transfers from one group within the economy, the taxpayers, to another group, the bondholders. Future generations inherit tax liabilities, but they also inherit bonds and the right to receive the interest on them.

Even if the debt had to be paid off, future generations, as inheritors of the bonds, would be making payments of the principal to themselves. In fact, of course, the federal debt never has to be paid off, any more than the debt of any going concern, public or private, has to be repaid. As parts of the debt come due, they can be repaid with fresh borrowings. Continuous refinancing is typical of the modern successful corporation, because confidence in the company's ability to earn future income makes holding its bonds both safe and profitable. Similarly, confidence in the continuing viability and taxing power of the federal government eliminates the need for net repayment of principal, either currently or in the future.

The Real Burden of the Debt: I

Does this mean, then, that each of us is $1,800 richer than we thought we were? Does every newborn infant start life with an unexpected bonus of $1,800?

Not quite, and therein lies the story of the *real* burden of the debt as contrasted with the imaginary burden.

In the first place, holdings of government bonds are not evenly distributed among the population. Some of us have more than our $1,800 share, much more; and some have less, much less. Thus current interest payments on the debt, while "only" an internal transfer from taxpayers to bondholders, may create problems of legitimate concern to the public. If bondholders are primarily in the upper-income brackets, and taxpayers are largely lower and middle class, the tax-interest payment transfer increases the inequality of income dis- tribution. Little is known about the pattern of interest pay- ments on the government debt according to income of the recipient. This transfer *may,* therefore, interfere with social objectives of reducing income inequality.

Furthermore, if the federal debt grows at a faster rate than GNP, tax rates will have to be increased in order to meet interest payments. Higher tax rates may reduce work incentives. If so, production falls and overall economic well-being decreases. In the United States, however, the national debt has actually declined, quite substantially, as a proportion of our gross national product. In 1945, the national debt was about 130 per cent of GNP; in 1955, 70 per cent; and in 1965, 45 per cent. Today, it is about 40 per cent of GNP.

Even if the debt falls as a proportion of GNP, if interest *rates* go up sufficiently then tax rates may have to be raised to meet interest payments, thus again possibly reducing work incentives. Interest rates have indeed risen since 1945, but nevertheless the interest "burden"—interest charges as a proportion of GNP—has not increased. Over the past twenty-five years, annual interest payments have been stable at between 1½ and 2 per cent of GNP.

The Real Burden of the Debt: II

Aside from the possible income-redistribution and work-incentive problems associated with interest payments on the national debt, there is one way in which the debt might impose a burden, a cost, on future generations. This involves not the interest, but the principal itself.

As we noted above, a country will become poorer only if it reduces its output of real assets, its ability to produce real goods and services. In this sense, a very meaningful sense, the wealth of future generations can be measured by the real capital stock they inherit, the real productive capacity of the economy we bequeath to them. A smaller capital stock permits less production, hence less consumption. A larger capital stock enables the economy to produce more, hence consume more.

Assume that the economy is already operating at a full capacity rate of production and that the budget is balanced. Whereupon the government increases its spending, financing its additional expenditures by sufficient new *taxation* to forestall inflation. In this case, the increased use of resources by the government comes primarily at the expense of consumption. Consumers, left with less after-tax income, have to cut back their spending by almost as much as government spending has been stepped up (a small amount of the tax payment comes out of saving).

Alternatively, under the same initial circumstances, assume that the additional government spending is *debt-financed* rather than tax-financed, and that monetary policy is used along with debt-financing to prevent inflation. Now interest rates will rise and the increased use of resources by the government will come primarily at the expense of investment instead of consumption. The higher interest rates will release resources from private investment for use by the government, with investment spending cut back by as much as government spending has been increased.

As a result, the building of new plant and equipment is curtailed, and future generations consequently inherit a smaller capital stock. Future productive capacity is lower than it might have been. In this limited sense, the "burden" of debt-financed current government expenditure is transferred to future generations.

Two qualifications are necessary. First, note that the argument assumes we start initially from a full capacity rate of production, roughly a full employment level of GNP. If the additional government spending were to take place during a recession, when there are idle resources available, then there would be no "burden" on future generations, no matter how it was financed. During a recession there are unemployed resources which can be tapped, so the government can increase its spending without anyone else reducing theirs. There would be no reason to permit a rise in interest rates, since the danger of inflation would be minimal, and an expansion in spending and GNP would be beneficial to all.

Under such circumstances, the future capital stock is not diminished. In fact, if the government's deficit spending succeeds in getting us out of the recession, the future capital stock will probably be *enlarged*. Thus increasing the national debt during a recession, instead of imposing a burden on future generations, is actually doing them a favor.

Second, the "burden" argument totally ignores what the government spends the money on. Assuming full employment, if the government's expenditure is for current consumption purposes—such as subsidizing inexpensive lunches for congressmen or schoolchildren—then total capital passed on to the future is indeed reduced. But if the government builds highways, dams, or increases any type of capital asset that raises future productivity, the increased investment by the government replaces the decreased investment by private business. Future generations will inherit the same capital stock, except more will be in the form of public capital and less in the form of private capital.

Moving from theory to reality, the fact of the matter is that about 60 per cent of our public debt stems directly from World War II military spending. In 1941 our national debt was $65 billion, and in 1945 it was $280 billion. Most of these expenditures occurred during a period of full employment. Yet few would call this a burden passed on to the future. Without it, we might well have had no future.

The Nuts and Bolts of Debt Management

Given a national debt of $360 billion, its day-to-day management has implications for the functioning of financial markets and for economic stability. How can the debt be refinanced most smoothly when portions of it come due? How much of the debt should be in the form of short-term treasury bills, how much in the form of long-term treasury bonds?

The dimensions of the Treasury's debt-management chore can best be appreciated by realizing that about $100 billion of the debt comes due every year, and must be paid off. How? By refinancing it, of course—that is, by borrowing $100 billion from someone else. The Treasury can replace the maturing issues with new short-term treasury bills, or with intermediate- or long-term bonds, thus providing some elbow room for altering the maturity structure of the debt.

In many respects, debt management is a close relative of open-market operations. The effects are very much the same, for example, whether the Federal Reserve sells treasury bills (which we call open-market operations) or whether the United States Treasury sells them (which we call debt management).

What are the objectives of day-to-day debt management? One goal is to minimize the interest cost of the debt to the taxpayers. But this can hardly be the only objective. If it were, the Treasury could minimize the interest cost—indeed, reduce it to zero—by simply printing money and buying back all the outstanding securities. That is, it could replace its interest-bearing debt (bills and bonds) with its non-interest-bearing debt (money). Obviously, the Treasury does not "monetize the debt," because to do so would probably result in massive inflation, and the Treasury also has the objective of managing the debt to promote economic stability. These two objectives often dictate opposite policy actions. Minimizing the interest cost suggests that when we are in a recession, and interest rates are low across the board, the Treasury should refund its maturing issues with new long-term bonds, thus ensuring low interest payments for itself well into the future. During boom periods, on the other hand, when interest rates are typically high, the Treasury should refinance by selling short-term issues, treasury bills, so the government does not have to continue paying high rates after yields have fallen to more normal levels.

Stabilization objectives call for just the opposite policies. When we are in a recession, the last thing we want to do is raise long-term interest rates, which is precisely what pushing long-term securities onto the market would accomplish. During boom periods, when we *do* want to raise long rates, is when we should sell long-term bonds.

Thus the objective of minimizing interest costs dictates lengthening the maturity structure of the debt (more long-term bonds relative to short-term bills) during recession periods and shortening the maturity structure during boom periods. Whereas for purposes of economic stabilization we should try to shorten the maturity structure during recessions and to lengthen it during prosperity.

One frequently used technique of debt-lengthening is known as advance refunding. The Treasury offers the holders of a selected security isssue, which still has a number of years to maturity, the opportunity to exchange their securities now for a new issue with a longer maturity. The investor receives a new security with a slightly higher yield without having to realize a capital gain or loss on his old security. This technique facilitates debt-lengthening by isolating the likely purchasers of long-term issues without the Treasury's having to resort to the open market.

Debt-management policy must be administered in co-ordination with monetary and fiscal policy. If minimizing the interest cost is the primary goal of the Treasury, then monetary and fiscal policy will have to take appropriate action to offset this counterstabilization debt policy. If economic stabilization is the primary objective of debt management, then the monetary and fiscal authorities can take this into account and reduce the forcefulness of their own actions.

Coordination between the monetary and debt-manage-ment authorities is also essential on a continuing basis because of the vast magnitude of the Treasury's refunding operations. When the Treasury refinances maturing securities, it frequently needs help from the central bank. If the Federal Reserve is pursuing a tight money policy, for example, it will often become less aggressive and resort to a policy of keeping an "even keel" in the money markets as the date of a refinancing approaches. In effect, the central bank will mark time for a while so that orderly money-market con-ditions prevail while the Treasury goes through the me-chanics of the refunding operation. It is difficult enough for the Treasury to roll over so much debt without being forced to cope with additional complications resulting from actions of the monetary authorities.

Monetary policy, fiscal policy, and debt management are often considered the three primary tools of stabilization policy. In practice, however, debt management has typically been the runt of the litter. Perhaps that is just as well. Given the power of monetary and fiscal policy to implement national economic goals, perhaps debt management can make its most significant contribution by successfully accomplishing the more limited but no less important task of continuously refinancing a very large volume of securities without unduly disturbing the nation's financial markets.

17

MONETARY POLICY:

AN OVERALL

ASSESSMENT

Is monetary policy important? Too much so, it would appear, to be left to the Keynesians. But we would also suggest that if war is too important to be left to the generals, by the same token money is too important to be left to the Monetarists.

Our exploration of the financial terrain has revealed a wide variety of ways in which monetary policy affects the economy. Let us devote the first half of this summary chapter to a brief review of the ground we have covered. Money does not influence virtually everything, as some Monetarists appear to believe. But neither does it influence practically nothing, as some Keynesians seem to think. Because monetary policy has not been completely effective does not mean it has been completely ineffective. (Evidently the most difficult position of all to maintain is a balanced one, without dogmatism or arrogance, admitting that many of the answers are not fully known and letting the chips fall where they may.)

Does more money always lead to inflation? No, but it can, under certain circumstances, and if the increase is large enough it probably will. Case 1: If the central bank expands the money supply while we are in a recession, then the increased spending it induces is likely to lead to more employment and a larger output of goods and services rather than to higher prices. Case 2: As we approach full employment and capacity output, increases in the money supply become more and more likely to generate rising prices. However, if this increase is only large enough to provide for the enlarged volume of transactions accompanying real economic growth, inflation still will not result. Case 3: Thus only when the money supply increases under conditions of high employment *and* exceeds the requirements of economic growth can it be held responsible for kindling an inflationary spiral.

The time horizon and the extent of inflation are also relevant. In the short run, an increase in monetary velocity alone, with a constant or even declining money supply, can finance a modest volume of inflationary spending. The longer the time span, however, and the higher prices rise, the less likely that velocity can do the job by itself. Over the longer run, the money supply must expand for inflation to persist; unless the stock of money is increased, the spending spiral that produces inflation will burn itself out for lack of fuel.

Conclusions: More money does not always lead to inflation (Cases 1 and 2), but sometimes it does (Case 3). In the short run, inflation can make some headway without any change in the money supply, but rising prices cannot proceed too far too long without the sanction of the central bank.

Are high interest rates always bad? No. They are not

immoral, they are not set by conspirators behind drawn blinds on Wall Street, there is no clear-cut evidence that they make the rich richer and the poor poorer, they have not sent the economy into a tailspin, and they are not responsible for inflation. They may be, in fact, just the medicine the economy needs under certain circumstances.

Does financial intermediation impair the effectiveness of a restrictive monetary policy? The evidence is mixed. It appeared to, until the mid-1960's. But since then the financial disintermediation that has accompanied tight money, due to both Regulation Q and the asset structure of the intermediaries themselves, has reinforced the effectiveness of monetary policy.

Is monetary policy discriminatory in its impact on residential construction? Undoubtedly monetary policy has laid a heavy hand on the housing industry. This is partly due to variations in the supply of funds reaching the mortgage market, primarily as the result of interest-rate ceilings of one sort or another. And to this extent, monetary policy does indeed discriminate against home construction. But it is also partly due to the response of potential home-purchasers to changes in interest rates, pulling back when interest rates rise and returning to the market when they fall. To the extent that fluctuations in residential construction are attributable to the interest-sensitivity of potential home-buyers, monetary policy has had a differential impact on housing but not a discriminatory impact in any meaningful sense.

Are stock prices affected by monetary policy? Not enough to use as a basis for placing a bet, but enough to at least keep tabs on what the Federal Reserve is doing. Until about five years ago, stocks frequently went their own way, regardless of what was happening to the money supply, and undoubtedly they will do so again. Nevertheless, in recent years there has been a much closer relationship between monetary ease and tightness and the ups and downs of stock prices, a relationship that is not likely to vanish in the foreseeable future.

Does gold matter? It is hard to see how, except insofar as we as a nation "psych" ourselves into it. Domestically it is irrelevant and internationally it is a nuisance. Monetary policy would work just as well (or as poorly), and money would be just as important (or unimportant), if all the gold stored underground in Fort Knox were returned to its native habitat in the bowels of California, Nevada, Alaska, South Africa, and the Soviet Union.

How effective is monetary policy in influencing GNP? It appears to have a significant, although not overwhelming, influence on aggregate spending within nine to twelve months. Much of this is due to its impact on residential construction, but business plant and equipment spending is also affected, as is state and local government spending and (indirectly) consumer spending.

Can monetary policy do the stabilization job all by itself? It could if velocity were stable or predictable. Then the Federal Reserve could induce virtually any volume of spending it wanted simply by adjusting the money supply to its known velocity. Monetary policy alone would be both necessary *and* sufficient to control GNP. Fiscal policy would be useless.

But the evidence lends little support to this position; velocity may not be infinitely variable or random, but from the record over the past fifty years neither is it reliably stable or completely predictable. And with a money supply of about $200 billion, a miscalculation of only 0.1 in velocity means a $20 billion swing in GNP. We have no choice but to use *both* fiscal and monetary policy. They are too closely interrelated to be able to use one without considering the other; to neglect either would be to invite trouble; and in any event neither appears capable of doing the job alone.

Even using both together, we have problems we have not yet been able to solve. The most important is our apparent inability to achieve full employment without simultaneously incurring a severe dose of inflation. Or, to put it the other way, our inability to achieve price stability without at the same time creating excessive unemployment. Thus far we have made little progress in resolving this conflict, and there are even some signs that it is getting worse rather than better. Nor does the problem seem to be confined to the United States. Every advanced industrialized nation faces the same difficulty, to a greater or lesser degree, and up to now none has succeeded in discovering a satisfactory resolution.

A Golden Rule for Money?

Although our most pressing immediate predicament revolves around the incompatibility between full employment and price stability, in the background lurks a related problem that also troubles many economists and policy-makers: Time lags make the implementation of monetary (and fiscal) policy potentially hazardous. For this reason, some Monetarists, most notably Milton Friedman, have abandoned countercyclical stabilization policy altogether. They never had any use for fiscal policy to begin with, and now the issue of time lags has led them to jettison countercyclical monetary policy as well.

Assume that the Federal Reserve forecasts a recession due six months from now. If the forecast is correct, and if a current expansion in the money supply would have an impact six months hence, well and good. But what if the Federal Reserve's crystal ball is not that perfect, and it takes over a year before the main impact of today's monetary policy is reflected in the economy? Then the effects of today's expansionary monetary policy are likely to be felt after the economy has passed the trough and is already on its way up.

As the diagram on page 197 illustrates, the impact of today's easy money may exacerbate tomorrow's inflation. This is Milton Friedman's explanation for the rampant inflation of 1969; the rapid rate of growth in the money supply in 1968, intended to forestall recession, lit the fuse of the inflationary time-bomb that exploded the following year. Tight money will have similarly delayed effects; it may be imposed with the best of intentions, to curtail a boom, but its real impact, being long delayed, might accentuate a recession. Monetary policy will be a destabilizer rather than a stabilizer.

On these grounds—the precarious nature of economic forecasting and the alleged length, variability, and unpredictability of the time lags involved—Friedman and some other Monetarists have given up on orthodox monetary policy. Friedman argues that the economy has been and is now inherently stable, and that it would automatically tend to stay on a fairly straight course if only it were not being almost continuously knocked off the track by erratic or unwise monetary policies. Conclusion: Quarantine the central bank. The best stabilization policy is no stabilization policy at all.

What he proposes instead is that the Federal Reserve be instructed by Congress to follow a fixed long-run rule: Increase the money supply at a steady and inflexible rate, month in and month out, year in and year out, regardless of current economic conditions. Set the money supply on automatic pilot and then leave it alone.

The specific rule would depend on the definition of the money supply adopted; increase the money supply by 3 per cent a year if it is defined in the conventional way as demand deposits plus currency, by 4 per cent a year if time deposits in commercial banks are added in as well. In either case, the particular number itself is not so important to Friedman as that once it is decided upon it be left alone thereafter. No tinkering!

The 3 (or 4) per cent figure is intended to keep prices stable and employment high by allowing aggregate demand to grow secularly at the same rate as the growth in the economy's real productive capacity. It is also supposed to compensate, according to Friedman, for a long-term gradual downtrend in velocity (although, in fact, velocity has done nothing but rise since the end of World War II, and from all indications it will continue to do so).

Such a rule, it is claimed, would eliminate forecasting and lag problems and therefore remove what Professor Friedman sees as the major cause of instability in the economy—the capricious and unpredictable impact of countercyclical monetary policy. As long as the money supply grows at a constant rate each year, be it 3, 4, or 5 per cent, any decline into recession will be only temporary. The liquidity provided by a constantly growing money supply will cause aggregate demand to expand. Similarly, if the supply of money does not rise at a more than average rate any inflationary increase in spending will burn itself out for lack of fuel. Anyway, any discretionary deviations by the central bank would interfere with the natural course of the economy and only make matters worse.

The Joint Economic Committee of Congress has been impressed enough to come part of the way toward a Friedman-type rule, in preference to permitting the Federal

Friedman's Alleged Perverse Effects of Countercyclical Monetary Policy

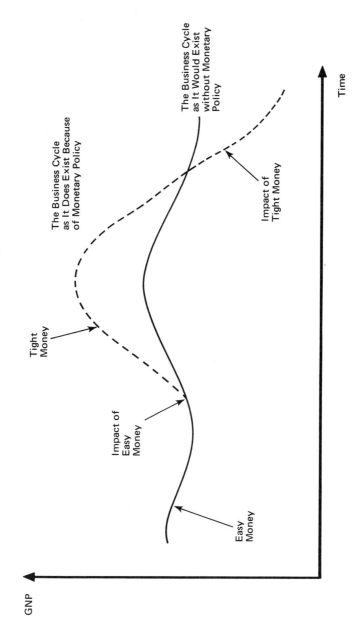

Reserve to continue using its own judgment and discretion in the conduct of monetary policy. Quite a few members of the committee are concerned that Federal Reserve "independence" has gone too far. As a means of somewhat reining in the central bank, the committee proposed in 1968 that Congress instruct the Federal Reserve to increase the money supply (demand deposits plus currency) by between 2 and 6 per cent annually. Thus far, however, their fellow congressmen have shown no great eagerness to enact the proposal into law.

The Friedman position is based on a number of pillars, each supported by mounds of statistical evidence produced by Friedmanites. However, very little is really known about the length and variability of the time lags. Such evidence as there is, and there is not much, is extremely mixed. Serious research on the subject is only in its early stages, and no consensus is apparent among economists who have worked in the area.

It is ironic—or instructive—that in the final analysis the extremists from both camps, Monetarist and Keynesian, have collectively ganged up on the Federal Reserve. The extreme Monetarists want to shackle it, because their concern with time lags leads them to believe it is both mischievous and harmful. The extreme Keynesians want to subordinate it to fiscal policy, because they think it is either useless or lethal.

In the middle, squabbling but making more common cause than they had thought possible, are the moderates: the moderate Monetarists, who believe that the forecasting-lag problem is not so great as to negate all the potential stabilizing effects of monetary policy; and the moderate Keynesians, who believe that monetary policy probably does change interest rates and/or the availability of credit and that those changes, along with fiscal policy, probably do influence spending decisions in the right way at the right time. While one concentrates mainly on the money supply and the other primarily on credit conditions, they are nevertheless in agreement that some form of countercyclical monetary policy is necessary and, on balance, beneficial.

It seems clear, after all is said and done, that central banking is still at least as much art as science. We simply do not yet know enough to legislate an eternal rule, or even a rule for the next six months, that the Federal Reserve must follow under any and all circumstances. When we do know that much, the Federal Reserve will know it too, and if they are rational men they will follow it regardless of whether it has been enacted into law or not.

Meanwhile, for better or worse, we have no alternative but to rely on our best knowledge and judgment in the formulation of monetary policy. We can only try to make sure that the decision-makers are able and qualified men (or women), with open minds and the capacity to learn from experience.

Epilogue

18

IS MONEY

BECOMING OBSOLETE?

What might the financial system look like in the year 2000?

Buck Rogers and Flash Gordon are passé, Jules Verne is old hat (around the world in *eighty* days), and *1984* draws too close for comfort. The science fiction of yesterday has become the reality of today. An excursion into financial science fiction for the Brave New World ahead should provide a fitting postscript to this book.

The Decline of Demand Deposits

"He spends money," they say, "as though it's going out of fashion." And perhaps money is indeed going out of fashion.

When checkbook money first began to gain popularity in this country, in the nineteenth century, it took decades before people finally realized what was happening. For a long time, checking accounts were not even considered part of the money supply. They were viewed as proxies or substitutes for "real" money, namely hard cash. Somewhere in the vaults of the banks, it was thought, nestled the coin and currency, dollar for dollar, behind every checking account.

As a matter of fact, even coin and currency were suspect. Dimes and dollar bills were considered mere stand-ins for the *really* genuine article—gold coin or bullion. That, and only that, was truly money. Anything less was, like Daylight Saving Time, a violation of the Lord's will.

Today, demand deposits are gradually losing their monetary importance, just as currency did a century ago. Checking accounts still constitute the bulk of our money supply, but the money supply itself has been diminishing in importance in our evolving financial system. Twenty-five years ago, the money supply amounted to half of our gross national product. A dozen years ago, it was equal to around a third of GNP. Today, it has shrunk to about one-fifth of GNP. We are carrying on more and more business, both financial and nonfinancial, with a relatively smaller and smaller supply of money.

Just as a hundred years ago coin and currency gradually gave way to the convenience and efficiency of demand deposits, so today demand deposits, as we have known them, are gradually giving way to even more convenient and efficient payment mechanisms. The growth of credit cards, for example, has made it unnecessary to write twenty-five checks when making twenty-five purchases. One check, at the end of the month, will do for all. And often that one check is not even needed. Your friendly neighborhood bank can make an automatic debit to your account at regular intervals, relieving you of the need to write even that one check.

If you have your paycheck sent directly to your bank by your employer, and make most of your purchases with that bank's credit card, with payment then settled up at stated intervals by the bank automatically reducing your account by the amount of the charges incurred, you will soon find your checkbook obsolete.

If we combine the essence of this already realistic payments system with the potentialities of the high-speed computer, magnetic tape storage, remote feed-ins, and satellite transmission, it does not take too much imagination to make a stab at the shape of things to come.

Debits and Credits in the Year 2000

A few decades from now, coins will probably still be with us for inserting into vending machines that we can then shake and bang to release our aggressions. But checks may well have vanished as quickly as they came. Check payment, after all is said and done, is nothing more than a book-keeping operation to begin with. As a method of information dispersal as to how the books should be kept, checks are—in light of present and foreseeable technology—notoriously cumbersome, slow, unreliable, and inefficient.

More in keeping with the twenty-first century will be a vast nationwide balance sheet and clearing system, in which debits and credits can be rung up virtually instantaneously by electronic impulse. Every individual and every transacting organization of whatever sort will be tagged at birth with a number and a slot on the "books" of a computerized nationwide accounting and payments system, a National Ledger as it were.

Credits and debits to each individual account will be made by the insertion of a twenty-first-century version of a

credit card into a twenty-first-century version of a telephone
or teletype. Instead of a written piece of paper instructing a
bank to credit this account and debit that one—that is, a
check, with its necessary physical routing from place to place
—the insertion of a strip of metal into the appropriate re-
ceptacle will automatically debit and credit both accounts
instantaneously. It should not be too difficult to devise a
system whereby the proper code will serve as a means of
verifying the validity of the electronic instructions to the
Great Master Bookkeeper in the Sky.

Eliminating checks would be only one of the many
advantages that would emerge from such a system. All
financial assets are nothing more than a representation of
someone else's liability or evidence of equity. Current practice, which consists of inscribing same on embossed parch-
ment, has been absurd for at least two generations. There is
no need for stocks and bonds to look like Pronouncements
of State by King Henry VIII. As everyone is fully aware, a
simple computer print-out would do just as well. However,
by the year 2000 even that will not be necessary, since it will
all be recorded automatically on the magnetic tape of the
National Ledger as soon as a stock or bond is issued or a
transaction made.

An even more important advantage will be the saving in
time and effort currently devoted to keeping the books in a
society slowly but surely being inundated by paper work. We
are only kidding ourselves if we think we have made much
progress in this area since quill pens replaced whatever it was
they replaced.

In any event, manpower will have to be saved somewhere
to provide personnel for the army of computer repairmen who
will in all certainty be busy around the clock answering
customer complaints and fixing breakdowns in the equip-

ment. One supply source for repairmen, of course, will be the cadres presently known as the Monetarists. Their hard-learned skills will be obsolete in the twenty-first century. After spending a lifetime accumulating regressions and correlation coefficients to prove that the money supply is the sole determinant of all plant and animal life, what else will they be able to do when money itself becomes no more than a historical *curiosa*?

A National Ledger payments system will be possible in a surprisingly few years. Already its introduction depends more on costs and financial evaluations regarding its profitability than on purely technological considerations. It remains to be seen whether the necessary services will be provided by one firm, by an association of private financial and nonfinancial firms, or by the government, alone or in partnership with private enterprise.

There are obvious advantages inherent in it being a governmental function. For example, as matters now stand, employees of the Communist Party USA are not permitted to receive social security benefits. If they and other malcontents could also be denied access to the National Ledger, and thus barred from making or receiving payments of any sort, the American Way of Life could be made even more Secure.

Implications for Financial Markets

With methods of communication and the dissemination of information perfected to the ultimate degree by the year 2000, in all likelihood financial markets will finally take on the characteristics of the purely competitive markets that economists have been talking about in classrooms since the days of Adam Smith. Instead of simple buy and sell orders, or bid and offered quotations, potential buyers and sellers of financial assets will be able electronically to transmit complete demand and supply schedules to a central clearing computer, specifying the amounts of various securities they wish to buy or sell at a range of alternative prices.

Of course, this in itself would not be quite sufficient to meet classroom standards for a purely competitive market, since among the prerequisites for such a market is that the participants possess perfect foresight regarding the future as well as perfect knowledge of the present. But even that might be incorporated by feeding probability forecasts into the Giant Maw of the computer. Is it too farfetched to suggest that such forecasts might even involve some of the parapsychological techniques—like clairvoyance and precognition—currently under intensive study at some of our most prestigious universities and on several all-night radio programs?

Implications for the Economy

The "New Economics," Keynesian or otherwise, will also mean something quite different in the twenty-first century than it means today. Monetary and fiscal policy are far too uncertain in their impact for use in the Century of Efficiency that will follow the present Century of Progress.

By that time, all assets and liabilities as recorded on the National Ledger will be subject to increase or decrease by any given percentage by Executive Order, thereby instantaneously altering the wealth of every individual and every business firm in the country. If aggregate spending does not respond promptly in the direction and amount desired, furthur asset-valuation adjustments can be fine-tuned until the reaction on the part of the private sector conforms to what is deemed necessary to assure the Good Life for all.

Given human nature, this may possibly give rise to the problem of "valuation evasion"—that is, an illegal market in which assets are valued and transactions effected at prices other than those recorded on the National Ledger. The result would be the accumulation of unrecorded wealth for those involved in such dealings. If this gains currency, so to speak, an entire underground financial system—complete with (unreported) deposits, handwritten checks, and a subterranean check-routing network—is likely to spring up in opposition to the more efficient computerized and satellite-supervised official payments system.

The most effective remedy to prevent such undermining of the common welfare would be to bar all participants in Financial Subversion from access to the National Ledger. Practitioners of too-private enterprise would thus be consigned, along with employees of the Communist Party USA, to deserved financial ostracism as Subverters of the National Happiness.

Such a solution would have the self-evident virtue of safeguarding the Sinews of our Efficiency, while at the same time being consistent with the preservation of our Cherished Freedoms.

SELECTED READINGS

Data and Current Comment

A comprehensive source of information on monetary conditions, general economic trends, and the policies of the central bank is the *Federal Reserve Bulletin,* published monthly by the Board of Governors of the Federal Reserve System. An annual subscription ($6.00) can be obtained by writing to the board in Washington, D.C.

However, more sparkling comment and analysis are generally found in the Monthly Reviews of the various Federal Reserve Banks. The most useful and interesting are the Monthly Reviews of the Federal Reserve Banks of Chicago, Cleveland, Kansas City, New York (very austere), Philadelphia, Richmond, and St. Louis (Brand X). In each case, you will be put on the mailing list without charge if you drop a postcard to the public relations departments of the various Banks.

Books on Money and Policy

Two basic money and banking textbooks which are classics in the field are Lester V. Chandler, *The Economics of Money and Banking,* 5th edition (New York: Harper and Row, 1969) and Eli Shapiro, Ezra Solomon, and William White, *Money and Banking,* 5th edition (New York: Holt, Rinehart and Winston, 1968).

A standard anthology of readings on money and monetary policy is Lawrence S. Ritter, *Money and Economic Activity,* 3rd edition (Boston: Houghton Mifflin, 1967). An even better book by the same author, although on a somewhat different subject, is *The Glory of Their Times* (New York: Macmillan, 1966).

Three highly recommended advanced works are:

John G. Gurley and Edward S. Shaw, *Money in a Theory of Finance* (Washington, D.C.: Brookings Institution, 1960);

Milton Friedman and Anna J. Schwartz, *A Monetary History of the United States, 1867–1960* (Princeton: National Bureau of Economic Research and Princeton University Press, 1963);

Thomas Mayer, *Monetary Policy in the United States* (New York: Random House, 1968).

Keynesian ideas all stem, of course, from John Maynard Keynes, *The General Theory of Employment, Interest, and Money* (New York: Harcourt, Brace and World, 1936). A convenient summary of Milton Friedman's views on monetary issues can be found in his *A Program for Monetary Stability* (New York: Fordham University Press, 1960).

Studies of the Financial Sector

Some formal models used to analyze behavior in the financial sector are:

Stephen Goldfeld, *Commercial Bank Behavior and Economic Activity* (Amsterdam: North Holland Publishing Company, 1966);

Albert Ando and Stephen Goldfeld, "An Econometric Model for Evaluating Stabilization Policies," in *Studies in Economic Stabilization* (Washington, D.C.: Brookings Institution, 1968);

"The Federal Reserve–MIT Econometric Model," in the *Federal Reserve Bulletin* (January, 1968);

Frank de Leeuw and Edward M. Gramlich, "The Channels of Monetary Policy: A Further Report on the Federal Reserve–MIT Model," in the *Journal of Finance* (May, 1969);

William L. Silber, *Portfolio Behavior of Financial Institutions* (New York: Holt, Rinehart and Winston, 1969).

INDEX

profit expectations and monetary policy, 48–49
public construction expenditures and interest rate, 61–62, 63
purchasing power, of money, 1931 vs. 1969, 3, 4

Quantity Theorists, 43

racial tensions, in U.S., 151
Radcliffe Committee (England), 110
recognition lag, 53, 54, 55, 63; *see also* impact lag, time lag
Regulation Q, 113–116, 120, 192
"Reserve Report," 74–75
reserve requirements, for demand deposits, 13–15, 50; as monetary control, 65, 67, 70, 71–72, 73, 74
reserves, net free, 74–75
reserves, unborrowed, 74, 75, 76
Ricardo, David, 43
"Rock-backed" money, 152–154
Rocky Marciano Principle, 143, 144
Rogers, Buck, 203
Roosevelt, Franklin D., 8, 141
Ruth, George Herman (Babe), 3, 4

Samuelson, Paul, 4, 129, 130
Santayana, George, 42
savings deposits, growth of in commercial banks, 107; as money, 9; and velocity of money, 24–25
savings and loan associations, 104, 121, 124, 125; deposit-rate control, 112, 113–114, 121–122; deposits in, as money, 9; growth of, 107
Scandinavia, poverty in, 96
Shaw, Edward, 109, 144
Shaw, George Bernard, 94
small business, and investment spending, 60–61; and trade credit, 61
Smith, Adam, 208

Smith, Warren, 98, 99
socialism, creeping, 8
Special Drawing Rights, 159
spending: aggregate, 164, 208; consumer, and GNP, 165; consumer, and income relationship, 166; government, and GNP, 165, 166, 167–168, 171; investment, 60–61
Sporting News, 134
Sproul, Allan, 87
stock market: competition from bonds, 138; correlation of price changes and baseball strikeouts, 134; institutional vs. individual ownership, 129; margin requirements, 136; market value of all shares, 129; and monetary policy, 130, 134–139, 192–193; and money supply, 4, 5, 130–134; 1929 stock crash, 131–132; and 1966 credit crunch, 136–137
Strong, Benjamin, 87

Taft-Hartley Act (1947), 33
take-home pay, and inflation, 3–4
taxation: countercyclical, 43; and deficit financing, 174, 175, 176; and GNP, 165, 166, 167–168, 170–171; income tax surcharge, 4–5; 1931 vs. 1969, 3
time lag, and monetary policy, 60, 63, 194–195; *see also* impact lag, recognition lag
trade credit, and small business, 61
trade unions, and monetary policy, 98, 102
treasury bills, 15, 25, 56, 57, 114, 118; and discount rate, 67–68; yield of, as policy indicator, 73
treasury bonds, 15, 186

unemployment: black vs. white, 40, 41; and interest rates, 98–99; and price level, 33; rate of, 32; rate of, vs. price stability, 37–38, 40–41; *see also* employment

DATE DUE